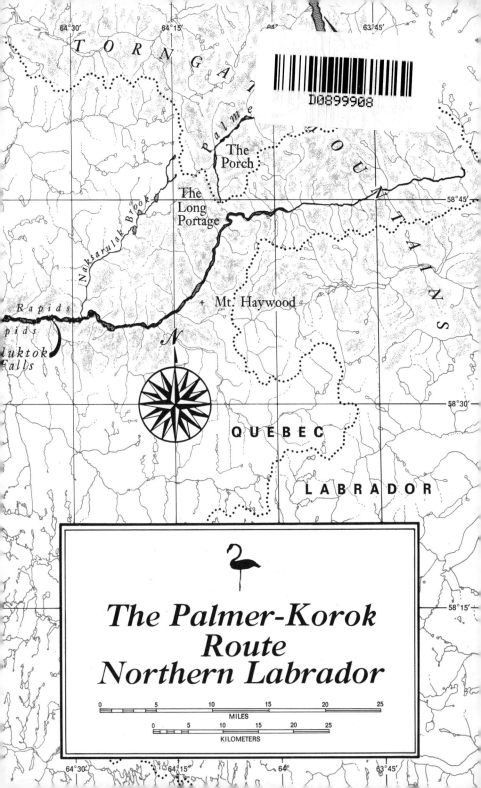

T O R N G A T

Palmer

The Porch

The Long Portage

Naksarulak Brook

Rapids

pids

luktok
Falls

+ Mt. Haywood

N

58°45'

58°30'

58°15'

M O U N T A I N S

Q U E B E C

L A B R A D O R

64°30' 64°15' 64° 63°45'

D0899908

The Palmer-Korok Route Northern Labrador

| 0 | 5 | 10 | 15 | 20 | 25 |

MILES

| 0 | 5 | 10 | 15 | 20 | 25 |

KILOMETERS

64°30' 64°15' 64° 63°45'

ALSO BY ROBERT PERKINS

The Boston Athenaeum
Art Exhibition Index, 1827–1874

AGAINST
STRAIGHT
LINES

AGAINST STRAIGHT LINES

~~~~

Alone in Labrador

by
Robert Perkins

Illustrations by the author

An Atlantic Monthly Press Book

Little, Brown and Company   Boston/Toronto

FIRST EDITION

Library of Congress Cataloging in Publication Data
Perkins, Robert F.
  Against straight lines.
  "An Atlantic Monthly Press book."
  1. Labrador (Nfld.) — Description and travel.
2. Perkins, Robert F. I. Title.
F1136.P47 1983   917.18'2044   83–1016
ISBN 0–316–69930–6 (pbk.)

The I Ching or Book of Changes. The Richard Wilhelm translation
rendered to English by Cary F. Baynes. Bollingen Series 19.
Copyright 1950 © 1967 by Princeton University Press. Copyright ©
renewed 1977 by Princeton University Press. Reprinted by permission
of Princeton University Press.

"Meditations of an Old Woman," copyright © 1958 by Theodore
Roethke from the book THE COLLECTED POEMS OF THEODORE
ROETHKE. Reprinted by permission of Doubleday & Company, Inc.

The lines on page 121 are reprinted from "McKane's Falls," in
Divine Comedies by James Merrill, with the permission of Atheneum
Publishers. Copyright © 1976 by James Merrill.

The lines of Bashō are from JAPANESE LITERATURE by Donald
Keene. Translated from the Japanese by Donald Keene. Reprinted by
permission of Grove Press. Copyright © 1955 by Donald Keene.

ATLANTIC–LITTLE, BROWN BOOKS
ARE PUBLISHED BY
LITTLE, BROWN AND COMPANY
IN ASSOCIATION WITH
THE ATLANTIC MONTHLY PRESS

MU

Designed by Dede Cummings

*Published simultaneously in Canada
by Little, Brown & Company (Canada) Limited*

PRINTED IN THE UNITED STATES OF AMERICA

To René and Joan Hague,
Shannagarry House

ACKNOWLEDGMENTS

The success of the expedition and the creation of the book itself are due to the indispensable help I received from many people, some of whom I'd like to thank here: Rodney Armstrong, David Bosworth, Kingsbury Browne, Rev. Robert Bryan, Frank Campion, George Cowley, Edward Cunningham, Veronica Cunningham, Richard M. Feldman, William Fitzhugh, Mari Funke, Jonathan Galassi, Edward E. Gray, Rebecca Gray, Dr. Kenneth Gregg, Lin Harris, Austin Hoyt, Hamlin Hunt, L.A.C.O. Hunt, William Knot, Steven Loring, Chuck Luckmann, Walter de Maria, Johnny May, Eric W. Morse, Robert S. Neuman, Noel, Bernard Peyton, Beekman and Elizabeth Pool, Barbara Roan, Judith Ross, David Saunders, Pete and Jean Shields, A. O. Smith, Craig Stockwell, William Vickers, Angus Whyte, Laura Willis, Robert P. Youngman, Arthur Zolot.

The following companies and organizations provided both financial and material help: Abercrombie and Fitch, The Boston Athenaeum, Buff and Buff Instruments, Dia Art Foundation, *Gray's Sporting Journal*, Harvard Square Art Center, Harvard Travelers Club, Ingram Merrill Foundation, L. L. Bean, *Outdoor Life*, Wabun.

ACKNOWLEDGMENTS

Special thanks go to the following individuals and organizations for their support and guidance: Dean Grey and the Old Town Canoe Company, Roger Furst and Eastern Mountain Sports, The Erewhon Trading Company, Upton Brady and the staff at the Atlantic Monthly Press, Sandi West and the Ossabaw Island Foundation, Doug Lewis, and Jill Moser.

Certain phrases, once you read them, never leave you. The phrase by John Berryman on page 191, for instance, has always pleased me. If in any part of this book I've trespassed without acknowledgment on another's phrase, or thought, the intention was not to plagiarize.

When three people journey together,
Their number decreases by one.
When one man journeys alone,
He finds a companion.

I copied this passage into my journal the night before I left Montreal. Half skeptically, I had asked the I Ching: What should I be aware of this summer?

LIST OF ILLUSTRATIONS

PART
ONE

~~~~~

"waterfall (wo' ter-fol', wat'er-),
n. a steep fall of water, as of a stream,
from a height."

WEBSTER'S NEW WORLD DICTIONARY

July 10, 1979. My ears just popped. Now I can hear my fire, hear the waterfall. No, the WATERFALLS. I can see five! None is less than hundreds of feet high. I'm near the mouth of the Palmer River at the foot of Nachvak Fiord at the beginning of my trip, several hours after the plane left.

I said the Lord's Prayer for the first time in a long time. Not out of fear of being alone, hundreds of miles from anyone, but as a way of saying thank you to the powers that got me here and the ones that, I hope, will guide me. I'm scared shitless.

Awed. All this space, so much space: a magnificent fiord leading to a valley rimmed by steep mountains, the Torngats.

The Torngats, larger, and stranger, than any mountains I've ever seen. Geologically, they're young, which makes them look massive and old.

No. Start over.

Where to begin? How to start?

At my feet. Rocks. It's all rocks. Reds, greens, browns (every chocolate color), gray, blue, gold. A land of rocks. A silent land. An immobile land. Only the water moves, the ocean, the river, the waterfalls. Lines of driftwood and seaweed mark the ocean's high tide around me.

In front of my foot is the perfect contrast to the mountains and the valley, a small group of delicate purple flowers and some cactus-looking plants. They've been submerged by the incoming tide. The flowers look as they would on land, except they're swaying under two inches of salt water! A land of sharp contrasts. The chubby cactuslike plants have little beads of oxygen clustered on each leaf, which makes them appear like precious jewels.

Beyond them stretches a generous sweep of bay, a level plain of water coming around a corner. Across from me the bay meets the mountains at a right angle. No delicate, gradual rise to the heights: it's all verticals headed straight for heaven, built from one boulder piled on another boulder, packed with an overwhelming detail of rocks. The colors change as I look toward the top of the mountains, from light browns and reds to more somber grays and bruiselike dark browns. Streaks of white snow, patches and gobs of it, cover the mountains. Even down to the water there are patches. I can't imagine the huge contraction involved in creating the Torngats. All that violent force creating this cumbersome, frozen monument to itself.

Pouring in above the mountains, the waterfalls. They are the one solid sound. Floating, suspended between heaven and earth, they are different from the sea, different from the river in its glass-smooth swiftness; but like the river, the waterfalls keep their course, always replacing themselves by succeeding hordes of water.

The sun has left the valley floor. I watch the harsh, unrelenting line of shadow creep up the mountains opposite.

The plane flew into this silence, this dream, an orange,

angry-sounding leaf falling in loud, tightening spirals to the fiord. After the plane left I tried to go fishing. I walked toward the river's mouth, took a few casts, sat down, and laughed. How can I be in such a place and fish? I can't concentrate. My eyes can't stop looking. I want to be walking in this landscape, a visual sponge soaking it all in. I came back to my gear and made camp.

It's hard to find a place among all the rocks for the tent.

I'm looking at *Monkey*, my canoe. I could say I named it that because it's small (fourteen and one-half feet long, thirteen inches deep, twenty-eight inches across), agile, fast, and clever like a monkey, but that's not completely true. It's named after the main character in a Chinese folktale, *The Monkey King*, a story written in the sixteenth century by Wu Ch'eng-en. These are the oral tales of demons and supernatural powers that Wu Ch'eng-en had heard as a child and wrote down as an old man. They focus on the outrageous adventures of the Monkey King during his journey with the monk, Tripitaka, to India to receive Buddhist texts for the Emperor of China. Monkey is always saving Tripitaka from demons, disasters, and death. He has little respect for hollow conventions and evil. What he accomplishes he does with cleverness, humor, strength, and luck. By naming the canoe Monkey, I hope it will have all the attributes of its namesake. I'll need them. The Inuit, or Eskimos, whose land I'm traveling through, name their children with the same hope. They believe naming a baby after a departed relative invites the dead person's spirit into the child.

The Inuit have a belief about the Torngat Mountains, too. They are named after a Faustian spirit, the Torngat, who the

Inuit believe lives in a cave in the heart of the mountains. He has the form of a giant caribou. In the summer, when the cows come to calve and the bulls to wander, they sleep in his cave. The spirit is huge — so huge that each night when he stands at the mouth of the cave, not even the antlers of the largest bull scratch his belly as he enters between the spirit's legs. Although not evil, the Torngat is dangerous, to be respected. White travelers as well as Inuit have remarked how uneasy they feel traveling here. Right now, I feel uneasy, too. Don't know whether it's a feeling I'll get used to or not.

The noise of Fort Chimo: the cars, the trucks with no mufflers, the motorcycles, the planes are all now a dream. They're gone.

The sun has set, but it's not completely dark. I'm far enough north to be in summer's perpetual twilight. A rich quality of light, a light different from the white light of noon. It seems to last forever. Each contour, every color is heightened in this oblique, subdued light.

My ears popped again. I can hear more clearly the lap of small waves, my movements, the silence. The silence is a hum wrapping around everything. It is a silence made deeper by the sound of the waterfalls. This landscape is an eternal dream, or awake in a way I hardly perceive.

July 11.   These journal entries are like labels on bottles. Later they will remind me of what filled my days.

Just now, the sun peeked over the shoulder of the mountain. I have a shadow — and warmth. Everything is under a layer of frost. It is thick enough on *Monkey*'s bottom to draw my first picture in. I drew in a wavy line of triangles for mountains, a sun, a small, curving line for the river, and a tiny dot, which was me. I feel that small here.

My night was full of tossing, more dream than sleep. I'm still full of city confusion, plane, car, motor, and people noise. I had a nightmare about Fort Chimo. Saturday night: the streets are sparsely lit, sections of dark dirt road are framed by long rectangles of light shining out of doorways, windows. Silhouetted figures inside the houses cast flat shadows onto the street. An endless procession of flat, long, thin black shadows passes across the lighted sections of road. They seem to emerge out of blackness, into blackness. Every other house a party: voices, music, laughter, shouts, and banging mingle in the street with the shadows. Everyone drunk. Men, women stumbling into each other. Their looks blank, or wild. I wander around, trying to understand why I am there, what it means. An Inuit woman, drunk, short and beautiful, weaves up to me. What was she saying . . . ?

What snapped me awake was a *slush, slush, crush, crush, crush* sound. Tangled in half sleep, I was sure I was being surrounded by twenty huge polar bears. This is it . . . the end. The least I can do is put my pants on. I unzip the tent door. A hundred yards away are eight caribou pacing over the small stones and wet muck of low tide in the fiord, not the bears I feared. I watch. They move slowly in fits and starts. Their heads bob as they move. Their color is the mountains, even to their white bellies, which resemble patches of snow. Truly, they seem to be mountain spirits who have gathered a few colorful rocks, a little snow, and transformed themselves into caribou to be able to move about better and convene with other spirits. Among them is an all-white caribou. He must be a high-mountain spirit.

I've finished breakfast: six slices of slab bacon and a cup of coffee. I have a quarter slab with me and won't do any hunting until it's gone. The tide is in. Now the eight caribou are sixteen, each one's reflection travels with him. The water mirrors the mountains the same way: each peak sweeps down to the shore, then sweeps back up again: one image substantial, one reflection.

I took Mandy's red-and-white wristband out. She'd crocheted it for me for luck. She was offered a summer job at the American Academy in Rome and took it. Rome. I can't imagine a place more different than here. I wonder how it will be between us when we are back together.

After breakfast I read awhile in *Camping and Woodcraft*, written by Horace Kephart and first published in 1916. It's the one book I bring on my trips. He has a certain way of describing his knowledge of the woods. Reading him, I always find something new. Today, I found this passage about traveling alone: "To the multitude whether city or country bred, the bare idea of faring alone in the wilds for days or weeks at a time is eerie and fantastic: it makes the flesh creep. He who does so is certainly an eccentric, probably a misanthrope, possibly a fugitive from justice, or likely some moonstruck fellow whom the authorities would do well to follow up and watch."* It was how he liked traveling best.

I wouldn't call myself a fugitive, an eccentric, or a misanthrope, but I have always appeared a puzzle to my parents and felt an outsider to my peers. I'm a little thickheaded. I could never take anyone's word that a fire would hurt me — twice as a kid I was pulled out of one with second-degree burns. I'd say that's partly why I'm here: just to see what it's like. Something no one can do for me.

---

* Horace Kephart, *Camping and Woodcraft* (New York: Macmillan, 1916), vol. 2, p. 146.

Evening.   After packing up, I paddled *Monkey* across the fiord. I climbed out on a snowfield, one of those small-looking white gobs I saw last night. It's at least six feet thick at the water's edge and must cover an acre! The scale here is deceptive.

For the second day the sun is bright. It unravels over the surface of the water, or appears as chips of gold lying there. If I had a broom I'd be a wealthy man. In the middle of the fiord the water is a deep, rich blue color. Looking down into it, I could see the sun's halo as I used to see it in the ocean as a kid. A blue like that makes me think of a title of one of Carl Sandburg's stories, "Only the Fireborn Understand Blue."

Everything is bold. I have to crane my neck to look to the tops of the mountains.

Back in the canoe, I paddled to the mouth of the Palmer River. I'd forgotten I couldn't just paddle upriver. From the plane it looked flat and crystal clear. It's still crystal clear, but it's not flat. The water's too shallow to pull deep strokes in and the current is too strong to paddle against. Today was my initiation into the fine art of lining a canoe upriver. If there were trees, I'd cut myself a pole, but there are none. It's all rocks. The only wood comes from small alder bushes growing in between the rocks. None of the bushes around me is over four feet tall. I'll be spending a lot of time gathering enough dead twigs and branches to keep a fire going.

Lining is like being an acrobat and a puppeteer at the same time. I hold two lines, one tied to the short thwart near the bow and one several feet forward of the stern. I stand onshore, or in the water. The bow faces upstream. By manipulating the two lines, I control the canoe in the current, can maneuver it around alders or rocks and along the bank so long as it is well-balanced in the current. There's hardly any strength involved as I walk *Monkey* forward. The challenge comes if I lose my balance or when *Monkey* is thirty feet away in the middle of the river and the current pushes it sideways.

Other times I'm in the water walking *Monkey* forward, holding onto the bow. My fear is losing my hold. I could slip, the current could swing the canoe broadside, tip it over, knock my feet out from under me. Any number of small mistakes could do me in.

I went about two miles and then gave myself the rest of the afternoon off. Made camp. Why not? There's no schedule here, except what I make. The water is cold. I'm walking in it a lot. I have to get out and wait for my feet and shins to thaw.

I made a camp under the soft curve of a knoll, one of the few gentle lines I've seen in this landscape. The grass isn't tall — it resembles a mown lawn, more rocks than grass, but still a lawn. Building a fireplace out of a few rocks is all it takes to make camp. I don't care how far from my "kitchen" I have to go to pitch the tent on a reasonably level and soft piece of ground. I brought *Monkey* up by the fireplace and put the wannigan and the baby nearby. At night I'll cover them with a tarp of rip-stop nylon. I brought an orange tarp in case I need to lay out a clearly visible distress signal. My tent is a yellow lightweight two-man tent. Between the orange tarp and the bright yellow tent, I have a corner on the market for brilliant colors here.

The wannigan is a plywood box, built to fit easily into the canoe. I built mine with screws. A few extra screws are always handy. The top lifts off. It can be used for a number of different things: a tray, a seat, a table for the stove in the tent. The box allows me to carry what I want in plastic bottles or cans: my cooking pots, stove, as well as more delicate items, which might get crushed in a soft pack. The wannigan's great advantage is how it makes bulky, sharp-edged, cumbersome items accessible and easy to carry. The disadvantage is that it's awkward in a portage. If the tumpline is too long the box hangs below the shoulders, cuts into my back, and adds extra strain on my neck. If it's too short the box rides too high and there's no room to extend my neck.

The wannigan has a shelf that rests on top of the bags and large plastic jars. Besides being where I keep the watercolor journal, the paints, the thumb piano, and Horace Kephart, it helps organize the kitchen utensils and other small items.

The baby is a canvas duffle carrying food staples.

The tumpline is a beautiful, basic piece of equipment. Just a length of half-inch leather, usually ten feet long, with tapered ends and a two- or three-inch headband in the middle. With it I can tie up and carry anything. Every culture has its version of the tumpline.

I use one to carry the canoe, the wannigan, and the baby. The baby carries the bulk of my foodstuffs, the things I don't use every day. I keep the current week's supply of food in the wannigan and food for the longer term in the baby. That way I'm not tempted to use more than I've allotted for the week.

After setting up camp I went ahead along the shore to scout the river and to fish. I love to fish. Although not as distracted by the view today, I am still overwhelmed and still adjusting to the landscape. Because I wasn't there, the fish weren't either. To fish well I have to be able to imagine myself into the water. Today, I couldn't do it.

The walk was over lots of rocks. I traveled up the river's right side. I was in the shadow of the mountains all afternoon, but across from me the sun spilled luxuriously over the face of the opposite peaks. Their scale is deceiving. They look closer than I know they are. The largest patterns of the geology — horizontal jags of color, the talus slopes, the scree, the different compositions of the mountains — stand out and make them appear simpler than I know they must be.

The alders grow thickest by the river. The distance from me to the ones on the opposite side of the valley blurs their individuality, makes them appear as one mass, green fingers reaching up from the base of the mountains.

Here the river is a braid of different streams meandering the last miles to the ocean. I climbed high enough to determine which is the main strand. No strand seems deep or wide, but that too could be deceptive. The water is unusually clear. The sandbars and rock bottom stand out sharply, making the river seem shallower than it actually might be.

Tonight I made the first frying-pan bannock: flour, baking powder, salt, dry milk, raisins, bacon grease. Ideally, I fry each side lightly to hold it together, then prop the frying pan in front of the fire and bake the bannock slowly to a golden brown. Mine fell apart, but finally most of the pieces got cooked. Julia Child would have thumbed her nose, but I enjoyed it — even the ashes and bits of tundra mixed in added flavor.

I carry a number-seven iron frying pan that weighs three and a half pounds. I could have brought a lightweight aluminum one. A friend, Beekman Pool, even tried to convince me I was crazy to bring an iron pan at all. To prove his point he weighed each on the scale. I still brought the iron spider. An iron pan conducts heat more evenly, but the principal reason is subjective — I'll be eating most of my meals out of it and I prefer the way food tastes cooked in one.

I bring everything I need: a home, clothes, food, even the spices I cook with. There's no hopping in the car for a run to the store because I want some tarragon. If I were walking the whole way I'd pay closer attention to weights and amounts. However, a canoe is a great beast of burden since it carries everything, except when I portage.

I've brought a plastic pink flamingo, something for the lawn. Tonight it's pitched in front of the kitchen. I bought it from a shop on Route 2 in western Massachusetts. I'd looked for one all spring, but didn't see one until late May. I thought about how to carry it. I couldn't afford to bring a whole three-dimensional flamingo, it would take up too much space. I put it in a vise and used a hacksaw to cut it down the middle. It's perfect. Half a pink flamingo fits into my pack and I can bend his neck around and keep small things in the hollows of his body.

July 12.   Woke early to piss. Outside the tent I saw a big, paper-white full moon in a deep Prussian blue sky. The moon glittered like a piece of ice. I went back to sleep.

It's still cold.

I should have a reason for being here. A purpose. Everyone I've ever met in the North has his particular reason, usually a scientific one. They're here to study or look for something. They're studying the fish, the birds, the bugs, the caribou, or the archaeology, or the geology, or the natives, or the weather, or the theology. Or else they're looking for something: miners looking for minerals, engineers looking for something to dam, hunters looking for a trophy, ministers and priests looking for converts.

What I'm studying and looking for is harder to put in words. I'm a generalist. If the scientist is like a botanist, I am a gardener. The search is not for material things as much as it is for an attitude or a quality of imagination. I am a painter. This trip is for my eyes, and what catches my eyes most are the waterfalls. Yesterday I saw two that started above the top of the mountain. They seemed like clouds pouring down the mountainside. No tops to them. It occurred to me, too, that waterfalls create the sound of the wind. I can imagine Remy Charlip, who writes children's stories, starting one with, "Wind never had any sound until it found a waterfall. . . ." If I see two waterfalls and one is behind me and one ahead, I'll hear the one in the direction the wind is coming from.

I enjoyed going down to the river this morning, filling a pot with water, and bringing it back to the fire. Realized this: first I saw the Palmer Valley from the plane, next I walked on the rocks, then I took some of this new world inside me with the water I drank. Now I have a whole day of memories in my head, and my skin aches from the wind and the sun, my body from the work of lining the canoe.

Yes, memories. I've brought so many from home. So much baggage. Perhaps because I'm alone I am more aware of them. Sometimes I can single one out but most often I have no control. My head is worse than the world's largest super-

Flamingo waterfall

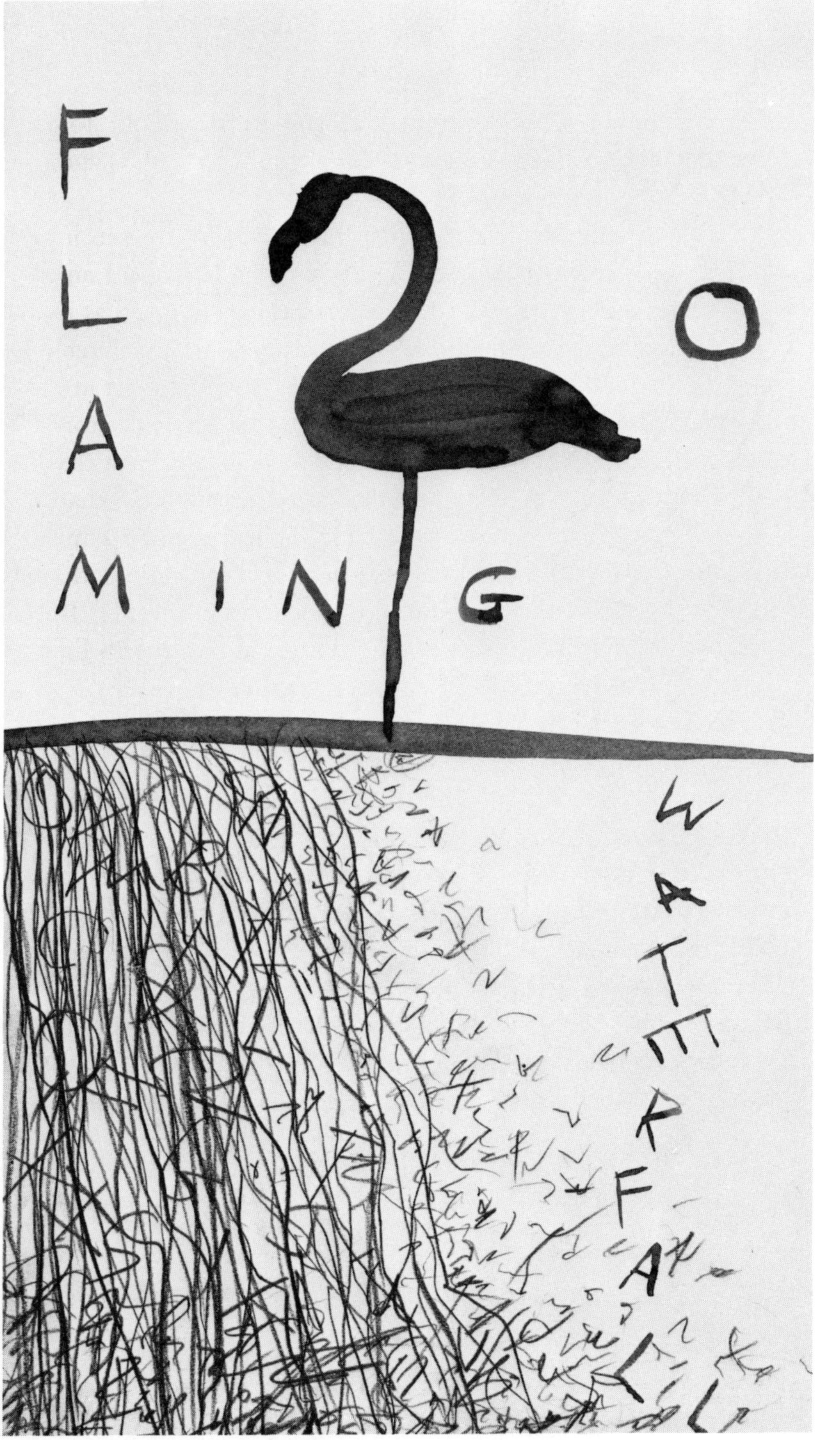
FLAMINGO
WATERFALL

market . . . after an earthquake. No, "supermarket" is wrong because it supposes original order. Can't an equation be made between wilderness and one's own wild interior? What I'm constantly aware of is how in an instant my mind travels over immense dream countries while my eyes and myself move over this reality like a tortoise.

I am thinking of Charlie Lee. We went to boarding school together. He was never happy there; neither was I. To settle his mind, Charlie works. If he's upset he goes to work. If he's happy he goes to work. If he's not sure what to do he goes to work. He was raised on a farm and lives on one now in Bakersfield, Vermont. He's no different today than he was twelve years ago. He works a lot.

When he and several friends had just moved to the farm, a group of us came to visit, disrupting the serenity of the house. After dinner, Charlie was nowhere to be seen. Outside a blizzard raged. We heard the tractor in the driveway. I went out and rode behind Charlie, even asked him above the noise of the motor and the storm what he was doing. He wasn't even giving the snow a chance to fall before plowing it. Over the sound of the wind and motor he yelled back, "I'm plowing my driveway. A man with a clean driveway is a man with a clean mind." So say Confucius Lee.

On my way here I spent a day with him before driving to Montreal. We traveled in his truck around Franklin County and shoed horses. He did eleven horses. We traveled through as many different towns, farms, residences, and saw as many different horses: skittish ones who wouldn't let him near them; good, solid workhorses; fancy jumpers; ponies.

It had been a cold spring and a late first hay. Everywhere people were cutting, tedding, baling, and hauling. The air was heavy with the hay smell. Charlie told me about the different people and farms we passed. He enjoyed knowing his place so well. The day was hot. The tiger lilies were in bloom, shots of hot orange in a green world.

Two images: first the cow. It's the ultimate symbol of civilization. It is completely dependent on man. The second image is of dogs. At every farm or house at least one dog hung around nearby until the shoeing was over so he could eat the clippings from the horses' feet.

I'm different from Charlie. His life goal is to become a dairy farmer. I prefer being a nomad, even within myself, traveling with everything on my back, or in the canoe. I prefer moving through a territory, not settling it. To see what life's like in this valley, to have the weather, the river, the waterfalls, work on me, enter me. To be like the river more than a rock. I like diversity, what is multiple, different. I like all that favors flow, and prefer mobile arrangements over systems. If it were possible I'd become pure verb.

There's been fog all morning. Now it's lifting out of the valley. Sun is darting through to highlight patches of river or mountainside. The fog has the look of gauze.

Across from me is a waterfall, white water dropping vertically over a horizontal stratification of mountainside. A great, big Barnett Newman Zip painting.

I carry a small notebook as a daytime thought recorder. My large journal I stow in the top of the wannigan wrapped in a plastic bag to keep it dry. The large journal is made from folding twenty full-sized sheets of watercolor paper in quarters. It's unbound. This gives me the option of unfolding a full sheet if I want to paint a large watercolor. It's Strathmore paper, made with a fiberglass core. I can write on it as well as paint on it. Because it's fiberglass it doesn't bend, but I notice when I'm writing that I pick up little particles of the glass in my palm. Like the journal I can write and paint in, I try and bring things that are multipurpose, though there is a long list of exceptions: the flamingo, the frying pan, the thumb piano . . .

I wouldn't bring a special "yoke" to portage the canoe. Except for that purpose, it's useless. I carry the canoe with a tumpline and two paddles. The tump stays on the canoe's middle thwart all summer, but if I need an extra rope, there it is. With the canoe inverted on top of my head, I can take the weight of it down my spine by using the tump alone, or onto my shoulders by allowing the paddles to take the full weight. By rocking the canoe's weight back and forth between the two, I can walk miles without putting *Monkey* down.

I always thought water ran flat and smooth. It's not the case even when it looks as though it is. The water reflects every rise or depression in the river bed. Being in it up to my thighs most of the time, my eyes are close to the water surface. In the morning sun the water around me is turned into a jangle of white gold. I can see each and every ripple in the river, tell where the rocks are, watch for the deep pockets (they're the calm-looking spots). The water's a skin and moves as mine does in response to what happens underneath it. I can feel the presence of the glacier that made the valley. Huge boulders appear in the oddest places. The rounded, scooped-out appearance of the valley speaks of a titanic crush of ice grinding its heel into the valley, creating it.

I've stopped to give my feet a chance to warm up. After half an hour they're numb. Slowly, I've gained some height climbing up the valley on a cushion of water. Rather, *Monkey* floats up the valley; I walk. It's cold water, thirty-eight to forty-two degrees. The dominant thing around me is rock. Colors: white, iron, gold, red, amber, and green. I'm looking at geological bone, the skeleton of the earth.

I came across a caribou skull bleached white, lying on green grass. It was a remarkable thing and a reminder: it could be me. I saw that some ants and flies were eating one last meal off it.

Have gained some more elevation. Can see back into Nachvak Fiord. On the left of the view is a mountain darker than those near me, whose profile is a man's neck and head as though he were leaning the back of his head on the earth. It's a striking profile equal to the Old Man of the Mountains in Franconia, New Hampshire.

Late afternoon.   I've turned the first corner. Can no longer see the fiord. The Palmer has stopped being a hundred little braided strands, but I've managed to find the one dead-end stream. The question is always how to proceed, and this time I went the wrong way. The main stream is to my left. On my way there, carrying my first load, I found a sandy point facing south. It's warm and protected from the wind by a six-foot-tall bank of alders. I made camp instead of continuing. If there'd been a group, I can imagine the endless discussion that might have ensued about whether or not this was the right place or the right time to camp. I've set the tent up against the alders, gathered firewood, organized dinner, and brewed a cup of tea, Lapsang Soochong.

A few mosquitoes have shown up as well as some small flies. So far, the small flies don't bite.

After dinner. I'm exhausted. I haven't established a rhythm. Everything is new. The scale, the activity. I haven't stopped giving out energy. I'm the goldfish in the bowl: I have to adjust myself to my space. I'm still expanding.

My hands ache. The last two days I've felt the two rings I wear. Rings are a nuisance in the woods. I wouldn't have brought them except they are talismans for me. One is a silver band, the other an aluminum marking band off a Canada goose.

The gooseband came to me at the end of my first expedition. In 1971, six of us canoed from Lake Mistassini up to the Eastmain River and down it to James Bay. We traveled two months to reach Eastmain Settlement, a village of two hundred Cree Indians and three Catholic nuns. We stayed several days waiting for the mail plane to come and fly us to Moosanee. After two months together we were tired of each other's company. We spent a lot of hours in the village, in particular with the nuns.

I'm not an admirer of Catholicism; it seems to me repressive, against the rights of women, and more against the individuals than for them, but I did respect these nuns. They lived on practically nothing, without church help. Their house was immaculate. They always had a cup of tea for anyone who wanted one. When they needed something they couldn't afford, they went to work for it. They had needed a chainsaw for their wood and one of them had gone south to a factory to earn enough money. Their faith was expressed through the example of their lives. They came from backgrounds as diverse as their nationalities: American, French, Spanish, and they were living in Eastmain, Quebec.

I talked with the sister from Spain the most, Sister Carmina. The day the plane came I went to say good-bye. She took me aside to wish me well and gave me the gooseband out of her sewing basket. Much later I realized I could wear it as a ring. It has a number on it recording the bird's banding and a Washington address. I've never sent in the number. I'm waiting. I want to let a few more years go by and see if I can't send in the number from an exotic place halfway across the world. I'd love to see the bureaucrat's face when he receives my inquiry.

Several years later I visited another group of Little Sisters to find out about the Sisters in Eastmain. This was in Boston where they live in an apartment in one of the city's worst slums. Half the apartments in the building are abandoned and trashed. Crime and poverty thrive. When I called they invited me to come for evening prayer and an early supper. The sister suggested I meet her at the Museum of Fine Arts. I didn't realize until I met her how close to one of Boston's pinnacles of culture is one of its worst slums.

They told me, due to the damming of northern Quebec's major rivers, including the Eastmain, the Eastmain mission was abandoned; my friends relocated to other communities around the world.

The twilight is wonderful. On each trip I take, my love for this time grows deeper. It's a soft, rich, sexual light. It lasts for hours, soaking each color, heightening each shape in the landscape. The raking light makes strong shadows. Each object is heightened by the darkness of its shadow. I usually tend to look at the object, not its shadow. It's the same as most people looking for the recognizable in a painting — their eye goes right to it. In both cases the negative space between the objects is nonexistent to them. I've grown to appreciate the shadows.

Rummaging in my pack, I've just found the six envelopes David Bosworth made for me. David's a writer. He works as a superintendent for an apartment building in Cambridge, Massachusetts. It's a good job, allowing him to spend much of his working day at his desk writing fiction. He felt on a solo expedition across northern Labrador I might like some outside thoughts. He gave me an envelope a week. Let's see what the first one says:

> A man, having looted a city, was trying to sell an exquisite rug . . . one of the spoils. "Who'll give me a hundred pieces of gold for this rug?" he cried throughout the town.
>
> After the sale was complete a comrade approached the the seller and asked, "Why did you not ask more for that priceless rug?"
>
> "Is there any number higher than a hundred?" asked the seller.
>
> Go higher . . . behold the human spirit.*

July 13.   Another beautiful day. Mosquitoes have arrived, but not too many. Body still aches. My face and the back of my hands sting from the amount of sun I took in yesterday. I have a small sore throat.

The day is fine. I'll neaten up camp, have another cup of coffee, and go fishing. Funny how I wanted to compensate for my fear by bringing more food. At home it was easy to imag-

---

* Robert E. Ornstein, *The Psychology of Consciousness* (New York: Viking Press, 1973), p. 85.

ine many disasters, and simpleminded wishing to think to solve them by bringing more food. Even at the last minute I was weighing other people's opinions. Richard, the photographer, visited me to go over the plan of his joining me for the last week on the river. He pointed out I had ten pounds of honey. Ten pounds! I could have fed the bears. Then, at Denny Alsop's I left behind several pounds of nuts and dried fruit.

My guiding factor for how much and what to bring has been the other two expeditions I've taken. Each one provided a different lesson. On the first trip, down the Eastmain, there were six of us. Through misjudgment we lost half our food with a month of travel left. We tipped the three canoes over in the runoff of Ross Gorge, damaging mine badly. For the next two weeks, until we accidentally came to a surveyor's camp, we were hungry. We became exasperated with each other. Being hungry made us edgy and unpleasant. We fractured into two groups of three, Denny Alsop, Nick Shields, and I forming one group. I never want to repeat the experience, even though those two weeks remain the most vivid of the trip.

Next I traveled with Bernie Peyton. We were retracing Captain George Back's nineteenth-century route from Great Slave Lake to Chauntry Inlet above the Artic Circle. We brought more food than we needed, including the makings of a Cordon-Bleu meal to prove that we didn't have to eat poorly in the tundra. Our idea was that even in the best restaurants the freshness of ingredients couldn't be guaranteed. We ate a nine-hour meal of as many courses, including freshly caught grayling, lake trout, ptarmigan, and a goose. We turned the canoe over and used it as our table. We had even bothered to bring several half bottles of different wines to have with each course: a sherry, a white, a red, and a Sauterne to have with dessert. We ate overlooking the river, a herd of grazing muskoxen on the opposite bank. We took rolls of film to confirm the fact. The irony was that our stomachs revolted at such a sharp change in diet, and we swamped the canoe the following day and damaged all the film.

This time we'll see. I have planned three meals a day, or one hundred and fifty meals. I won't ration myself. If I want another spoonful of honey, I'll have it. I wonder, though, if I couldn't get by on less. Part of the pleasure is not to be burdened; even food can be a burden.

The Erewhon Trading Company supplied me with the basics: short-grain brown rice, split peas, lentils, chick peas, steel-cut oats, honey, whole-wheat flour, cornmeal, miso, peanut butter, cheddar cheese, raisins, dried apples, prunes, millet, couscous, tamari, roasted cashews, kasha, sea salt, nori, mixed vegetable flakes, Familia, granola, sesame oil, tea. With a pressure cooker, converting the grains into filling meals is a snap. I could eat freeze-dried food, but I wouldn't enjoy it. I could eat a more selective diet, but I wouldn't enjoy that either. Five weeks is a long time, and with the variation and type of food I bring, I enjoy. Candy is good, too. I'm carrying some sourballs, and trying to train myself not to crunch them up right away, but to suck them.

While I was getting organized for fishing, to head toward the first Palmer pond, the copies of some letters fell out of my journal. Reading this one to Denny made me realize how quickly and easily the trip was organized. I didn't decide to go until April. I was driving to Montreal by the middle of June.

The Alsop Canoe Company
Ice Glenn Road
Stockbridge, Mass.

May 1st, 1979

Dear Denny,

I'm excited that you're building the canoe for this summer's expedition. I do agree, in many ways this is a wonderful combination of how each of us wants to work. With that canoe will travel so many of our past selves, our shared and unshared experiences and our dreams for tomorrow.

I'm terrified, Denny, but very excited as well. The rivers are well suited for a solo trip. The distance isn't overwhelming. I shouldn't be rushed. The water shouldn't be as heavy as the Back River was for Bernie and me. This is the right time to travel alone. My girlfriend, Mandy, is going to work in Rome this summer. The Athenaeum is letting me take time off from my job. My folks are nervous, but if I decided to wait for their blessing, I'd never go.

I've received nothing but support: Erewhon, Eastern Mountain Sports, Gray's Sporting Journal, Outdoor Life were full of enthusiasm and help. Remember how it was organizing our trip on the Eastmain in 1971? Nobody wanted to back us then. I'm enclosing our letter exchange with the man at Abercrombie's. I didn't know I'd kept it, but I did. Remember how mad he made us? How I returned the next day with our rough draft of a letter and copied it out long hand in front of his secretary, handed it to her thinking we'd finished with them. Then, that night, we regretted it because it seemed juvenile and arrogant.

Dear Mr. Z.,

You are a perfect example of the inhospitality which I have always heard typified New York. Not that you are not a smart man. You were kind and helpful during our meeting yesterday, but not very understanding.

On your recommendation, Denny and I stopped at the camping department to see if you had, or could get, what we needed. We felt that if anyone would have it, Abercrombie and Fitch would. For your information you do not carry pressure cookers and the reflectors you do carry are Palco reflectors, which we showed your salesman how to set up. They would not stand up to the trip we are taking. From talking to a buyer, we learned Abercrombie and Fitch would not possibly be interested in getting either of those items.

For the first time since the trip was conceived we found ourselves trying to sell it. If Abercrombie's did not feel we were doing as much for them as they were for us, then we are not interested in having them associated with our trip.

When we left your office, Denny and I thought back to a man who out of sheer curiosity came from behind his desk to kneel down at his coffee table and look at our maps and find out what we were up to. There stands the difference, as we see it, between National Geographic *and the Abercrombie's of today. You were right to say, as you said, that "your" store did not outfit Chichester, it was a store called Abercrombie and Fitch.*

We understand the position you must take today, and we understand National Geographic's. *The ability of operating on a handshake and a gentleman's agreement still exists and is the reason we do not choose to ask* Geographic *for a letter, on their letterhead and signed by them so that Abercrombie's "might" consider us.*

Anyway, I will remember you. We have your card and when, and if, we go we will send your card back with a copy of the story.

I have a friend in Goshen, Vermont whose mother just died at the age of a hundred and three. He always told me he never met an interesting man who didn't have a bite.

But he feels himself a more interesting man because he has always bitten back.

Sincerely,

Denny Alsop and Robert Perkins

P.S. *It has been my experience that Perkins is one of the easiest names to spell in the English language.**

Dear Mr. Perkins,
I have just finished reading your letter and find myself on the defensive. I do not enjoy defending my words, or justifying my actions but I feel it is necessary to answer you. Your letter is thoughtful, provocative, and written with deep emotion, but is it fair?
First, you say I am an example of inhospitality in New York. If this were so, would I have invited you into immediate discussion of your request, as is the case, or would I have put you off and told you to make an appointment (a good delaying device that was not employed).
Next you mention the eager interest shown in your project by National Geographic. *Of course they would show an interest. If your trip is successful, they have a story to tell that sells their magazine. Perhaps we wind up with a credit line somewhere in the story, if an assistant editor doesn't cut it out.*
But of course, all this is minor as far as A & F is concerned. After all, how many dollars would it cost us to contribute what you requested?
Then you resent my asking for a statement from National Geographic *on their letterhead because this implies my lack of trust in what you tell me. So, let's talk about the store and*

* In a contrary tone, Mr. Z had asked me to spell my name.

some of its problems for a bit. For the past two years A & F has lost a substantial amount of money. This is why it underwent a change in management late in 1970. And it is why I am here.

One of the figures presented to me upon my arrival was the dollar value of merchandise that A & F had donated or lent to various causes over the past few years. This amounted to over $50,000 worth of merchandise that would never be sold. It was either soiled, lost, broken or stolen. So what do you do about such a situation? You do the only thing you can do. You put a stop order on all such requests. Many of the requests are legitimate. But not all of them are. Some are from "promoters" who look for any contribution they can get and use it to their own advantage. Some are from plain old fashioned thieves.

Sure, what's a couple of bucks anyway? But add them up, here, there, and everywhere and it totals $50,000.

Of course, many requests are legitimate. O.K. so perhaps I'm interested. Why should I trust you? Because you talk intelligently and in a quiet voice? Why should I honor your request when I have turned away many others? What is my basis for breaking my own rule?

The answer is yes, I am interested in your request, and that is why I asked for a National Geographic letter . . . to assure myself it was a legitimate request and not another petty thief looking for easy loot.

You know, the management has its first obligation to the profitability of the company. This is not such a horrid phrase because we employ over seven hundred people and they have to pay their rent and put bread on the table just like you and I. So a little extra caution at my end doesn't hurt.

About ten minutes after reading your letter, my secretary gave me a folder containing copies of correspondence you have had concerning your journey. You will remember I had

*not seen any of this when I spoke to you yesterday. I am
satisfied with what I have seen, and no longer request the
Geographic letter.*

*If you still want A & F to participate, we will. If we
haven't got the merchandise you want, the pressure cooker
and the reflector, then go out and buy it and send the bill
to A & F, attention my name.*

*If your answer is yes, then call me person to person collect
at the store early next week. Whatever you decide, I do
wish you the best of luck on your journey. I know you
don't lack the courage.*

*One other thing, I'm lousy on names, good on faces, so
that is why I asked you to spell yours. I'll tell you one thing,
I'll remember the name Perkins for a long, long time.*

Yours truly,

Mr. Z.

*P.S. Please excuse my typing and spelling mistakes. This
is my own composition without a secretarial re-type.*

*Denny, I'll bring the same pressure cooker Abercrombie's
donated to us! I'll bring one wannigan, one baby, one pack. The
rough estimate on weight is: me, 190; wannigan, 85; baby, 50;
pack, 30; total, 355 pounds. These are maximum weights. That's
all the canoe has to float.*

*Strength, stability, flexibility, lightness are important adjectives
to bear in mind in the design. I hope you'll have a prominent
"A," or logo, on the boat that will help people identify your
work. These are a few thoughts I'm having while I'm writing.
I'm sure you're way ahead of me.*

*What is it that we're trying to keep alive in ourselves, living
the way we do? I know you haven't had an easy time of it with
your family. Neither have I with mine. They seem to feel we're*

against them and the values they stand for. I think they have it backwards but I hear it all the time. To desire to be an artist is seen as some kind of a threat. My father's even said to me they're second class citizens. He's such a hard-ass about certain things. I know he's wrong, I feel it in my bones.

There are five children in my family, three girls, two boys. Not one of us is living up to our parents' expectations. None of us have what's called a company job. Tom builds ocean racing trimarans; Flo is an artist; Eve is a clothes designer; Beau sells antiques with an expertise in porcelain. I'm a painter working part-time in a library. What exasperates the folks is our lack of interest in what they call security. They can't see how we're going to survive unless we're married, in a good nine to five job, a part of the system. Sound familiar? Neither of them have any inclinations toward art, or understand the type of lives we live. They're still scratching their heads wondering where they went wrong bringing us up. My father's latest rationale is that he wasn't strict enough. But they assume they made a mistake. I don't believe they did. We got the message, his and my mother's most important one: stand on your own two feet. It hasn't lined any of us up to receive vast financial benefits from the system — but neither have we had to accept the compromises of such a life. One of which would be not taking this trip.

The hardest thing has been not to talk myself out of going. I've been so caught up in the organization of the trip, I haven't thought much about the consequences. The other night I woke up in a cold sweat. In the morning I had what I thought was a case of pimples on my chest. They're hives. Anyway ...

I'll need a packing case for the canoe. It will be sent as cargo from Montreal to Fort Chimo. Depending on how I travel with the equipment, I could either carry the materials and build the crate at the airport hangar, or assemble it at Stockbridge.

This is my schedule: leave Boston for Stockbridge on June 29; arrive at Charlie's July 1st in Bakersfield, Vermont; go to Montreal

Monday to deliver canoe and equipment to Hangar Number Three (cargo has to arrive one week ahead of departure); leave Montreal on July 8 for Fort Chimo; fly from there to Nachvah Fiord on the first good day after July 10. Travel up the Palmer River, cross the divide in the heart of the Torngat Mountains, pick up my tundra turnpike card and enter the Korok River freeway down to Ungava Bay. Toward the last ten days of August paddle around the corner into the town of George River. Arrive home sometime in September.

Outdoor Life and Gray's Sporting Journal are paying for a photographer to join me, for the last thirty miles of the river. I don't like the idea, but they're paying for the trip. This is their guarantee of good action pictures.

Call me anytime, collect. The sooner the canoe is built, the more time I'll have to become familiar with it.

Love,

Rob

Later.   I'm walking high on the mountainside with a good overview of the river, trying to decide which side will be better to line the canoe up. I keep looking for that dark shape to glide or dart over a light-colored rock or a white patch of sand. I've seen no fish so far. The water is clear. It could be made of glass. Some pools draw me down to cast in them anyway, just for the sheer pleasure of it.

During my hike I've been thinking about Denny, our first trip, and my second trip with Bernie. I think of Bernie when I fish. My father brought me up fly-fishing, but not until I fished with Bernie did I see the elevated beauty it can achieve. Bernie is good. He has the same natural feeling for it that Paul has in Norman Maclean's story "A River Runs Through It." He has that same magic. He seems to know where the largest fish are and how to catch them. I saw him astound an expert English fisherman in Ireland by catching the only salmon of the week on a homemade fly called a "Woolly Worm." This was something the Englishman had never heard of, nor had he ever seen anyone catch a good-sized salmon on his river with a dinky-looking six-foot trout rod.

A piece of the landscape, until now only a view, became real today. I've spent the last hour struggling through one of those green triangular swaths that reach to a point high on the mountainside. Bastard willows! If it weren't for the caribou the going would be even tougher. The animal trails meander across the landscape. They resemble a careless line an artist makes on the top of a meticulously rendered landscape. I see them where they've worn down the grass. Often I can find a path they've made through the willows, but their paths are very inconsistent. I'll be following one and it stops. Or I miss the turn and plunge into the willows over my head. The willows are dense enough in places that for yards and yards my feet don't even touch the ground. The alternative is staying on the rocks, skirting the willows. The rocks are just as hard to walk over, and to stay out of the willows means climbing higher up the mountainside.

Evening.   I reached the first Palmer pond, walked right out onto a small sand beach. No problem with firewood when

I camp there, lots of driftwood. A set of wolf tracks in the sand ran the length of the beach. I imagine I'm watched more than I know.

On the way home I went high, too high. The way back became much longer, the rocks unstable. I scared myself. I started scrambling and pushing through the willows. I got through one clump to find I had only half my fly rod. The leader and line I had reeled up to prevent them getting tangled in branches, but I hadn't thought to break the rod down. The top half had been pulled off somewhere behind me. I had a flash of panic. Look for it? Abandon it? Would I find it? I retraced my steps. No luck. Was it flipped away from my trail? Or hung up in the willows, looking like a branch?

Finally, I found it resting across two branches close to where I'd realized it was missing. The branches held it like two arms presenting me with the tip. I can't afford to be careless with my equipment, it's all I've got.

A second lesson was brought home to me crossing a rock patch by a waterfall. I was walking on a steep pitch, taking long steps, one flat rock to the next. The rocks were light orange, red, and white, beautiful-looking and treacherous. Stepping onto a rock, it moved, springing loose a larger rock, which fell across my foot. The size of a Volkswagen, it grazed my boot and was stopped from mashing it by a third rock. Like a bear trap, if it had caught my foot not only would it be broken, but I'd have been trapped. I'd have looked foolish when they found me, if anyone found me. The only thing in mint condition would be my spiffy Gortex raincoat.

Walking down the last slope, stopping to rest against a boulder, I watched the play of late afternoon sunlight on the alders. I felt glad to be alive. The light created dark hollows of shadow in places and heightened the mountains' colors in

34

others. I took a picture of my tent. I don't take a lot of photographs, but I could see the tent down below me, a minute yellow spot in front of a bank of green alders. The river flowed by next to it. I felt glad to see my home.

Then I noticed the spider webs. At this angle of light I could see hundreds of them as if they were covered in dew. To think, all those spiders, spinning their webs, patient as fishermen waiting for a strike. I hope they had better luck than I did, but I doubt it. There haven't been any insects yet. It's still too cold, too early in the season for the earth to have warmed up enough. Although in the last two days I've been feeling it happen. After the sun's been out a few hours the heat rises off the land in waves.

The rocks by the river are rounder than those on the mountains. A sensual treat is to put my hand on a smooth, round rock that's been lying in the sun. The retained heat makes it seem like a gigantic egg. There are fields and fields of these rock-eggs. It would be unnerving to be here when they hatched.

From high up the mountain, the Palmer River appears minute, delicate, and the Torngats seem like older brothers protecting their virgin sister, the river. After today, I think I'll stay down here with her. I can see Johnny May, the Inuit pilot in Fort Chimo, as we stood on the tar runway, after he'd said good-bye, turning back toward me to say almost as an afterthought, "Be careful."

I had been given Johnny's name as the person to fly with. I flew in his plane, but the pilot was his half brother. That afternoon's flight in the Beaver from Chimo to Nachvak was nothing like the flight up to Chimo. The small Beaver skidded around on the rough air, hung suspended in its deafening noise, stayed close to the land. We had a clear view of the coastline, the green dots of the tamaracks, the lighter, larger green patches of the moss, the distinct contours of the countryside, and the meandering lines of animal trails. The Torngats rose in front of us to the east. Flying close over their tops, we looked into huge bowls of snow, watched the shadow of the plane shrink and expand and ripple as it reflected our progress.

In contrast, the jet from Montreal was one smooth arc. Airborne, we climbed above a cloud bank to fly between a uniform blue sky and a white cloud ocean. Not until we dove through that white sea and appeared on the other side did the emerald and earth colors of the land around Chimo appear. It was overcast. The wings of the jet made vapor trails as we landed.

Outside the plane it was warm. A few lazy mosquitoes appeared. I asked where I'd find Johnny May. In his hangar over there. I found him putting training wheels on his daughter's bike.

He and his wife, Louisa, put me up before I left. I was surprised to find Johnny complained about business and paperwork, and that Louisa had her hands full with three children and the housework. They both kept an eye on the clock. They appreciated the time ahead of me just as much as I did. A time to sleep when tired, eat when hungry, and have the option of taking a day off when I felt like it. I had imagined things to be different than they were in Boston, but they weren't.

Another expectation that proved wrong was my idea that people in the North would understand my trip. Johnny and Louisa were an exception. Most people thought I was crazy. One curious man drove out past the town dump to my campsite by the lake. He didn't say anything. He walked around shaking his head, looking. Finally he laughed, seeing the name on the canoe, and said, "I hope it doesn't make a monkey out of you."

❧

July 14.   Didn't sleep well. Scared myself yesterday. Came home, had a stiff rum and iced tea, too large a dinner, and tossed all night. Bad dreams.

Near dawn I heard a bird waking up. One bird. It wasn't nearby. I listened to its beautiful song of long, drawn-out notes piling up on top of each other. High notes sometimes seeming to overlap each other. The delicacy of the sound made me feel the immensity of the valley, the quietness of the dawn, the wildness and indifference surrounding me. One small bird and his song reassured me; a bird that would easily fit in the palm of my hand could fill miles and miles of this immensity with its song, calling the valley back from the night.

I felt even better after a few pancakes, some bacon, and a cup of coffee. If I harbored doubts about the quantity of food I'd brought (and I did), I don't anymore. After almost getting stuck under that rock, I thought about starvation. What would it have felt like to starve slowly with my foot caught under a rock?

Starving is a possibility. It has always been, in the North. Indians and Inuit take it in stride. The journals of the European explorers are full of it. At first, the Europeans weren't very intelligent. They clung to their habits, which prevented them from learning from the natives. One expedition, starving, desperate, and exhausted, ran into a family of Inuit hunting on the ice. The Inuit offered to help them. They speared some seals. The Europeans took the seals, ate the meat, but left the guts. The Inuit took the guts. Unfortunately, the Europeans needed the vitamins and enzymes in the internal organs more than they needed the meat. Most of them died from scurvy, or malnutrition, because they did not understand this.

Labrador has its cases of starvation. In the early 1900s, Leonidas Hubbard starved on an overland journey. His wife Mina's account, *A Woman's Way Through Trackless Labrador*, is a sad but fascinating story about her search for her husband. More recently, in the thirties a Mr. Kohler, due to an argument with his companions, set off on his own and died. Even the Korok has its story. During the mid-sixties two men died of starvation on the lower reaches of the river, and I imagine more deaths than these have gone unrecorded.

Even Captain Back, who was such a successful expedition leader, began his career in the Arctic on an expedition where half the men were killed by starvation, or exposure.

As a thirteen-year-old midshipman during the Napoleonic wars, Back had been captured and put in a French prison. There he developed his skill as a draftsman. This ability gained him his first commission, in 1818, with Sir John Franklin, to be one of three officers accompanying him into the Canadian Barrens on the overland journey to the Coppermine River and the Polar Sea. On the return journey from the mouth of the Coppermine River to winter quarters at Fort Enterprise, half the party died of cold and starvation. The others owed their survival to Back. He was sent ahead with the healthiest men, and was able to keep them moving until he procured help from the Copper Indians. Franklin and three others were barely saved; they had been existing on old caribou hides and gnawing on bones.

Ironically, years later Back was an unknowing contributor to the total disaster of Franklin's last expedition. With two ships and one hundred and ten men, Franklin left England in 1845, confident that they would be the first men to find the Northwest Passage. After five years, when no word had been heard, concern mounted at home. A controversy broke out in the London newspapers as to where a search should be centered. By now Back served on the Board of the Admiralty, in whose hands the decision rested. Back discouraged the idea that Franklin would abandon his ships to reach the mouth of the Great Fish River, the river Back himself had explored in the 1830s. He felt his exploration had proved that the river wouldn't have been a viable escape route. Unfortunately, this is exactly what the survivors did attempt, but not until 1855 was conclusive proof found.

This was when James Anderson, Chief Factor for the Hudson Bay Company, found relics from the Franklin expedition among the Inuit living at the mouth of the river. Their most gruesome discovery was that of two skeletons in a long boat, thirty-five miles from the inlet leading to the Back River. There was ample canned food in the boat. Evidently scurvy had been the cause of death. More recently, other parts of the story have been pieced together, and I can imagine the one hundred and ten men moving slowly down the coast of King William's land, abandoning small groups of their comrades as they became too weak to continue. Saying as they left them that they would return soon with help, knowing full well that was the last they would see of them.

I was hungry on the Eastmain. Also, Bernie and I reflected on Captain Back and the Franklin tragedy at the end of our 1976 trip. We spent three cold hungry days at the abandoned nursing station in Chauntry Inlet, waiting for our chartered plane to come from Yellowknife. Not only had Back come down his river, he had to return up it — all the way back to

Fort Reliance. We were mere tourists in comparison, but after nine weeks in the tundra we were tired, the snow had begun, and we were pushing the limit of our emotional and food reserves.

On our final morning it was so cold we hardly wanted to get out of our sleeping bags. We expected the plane to descend that day from the gray, snow-filled clouds. We began thinking about the pilot and copilot who would be our first people-link with civilization. Listening to the wind shake the tent, we thought of the plane flying out of Yellowknife. *Yellowknife* — the mere sound of the word conjured up images of luxury: a warm, clean bed, an unending hot shower, a hot cup of coffee, even the six-hour flight in the plane sounded good. We imagined the pilot waking up in his warm bed, eating breakfast at a table, preparing a hot thermos of soup or coffee for the flight.

I think about food a lot in the tundra.

We asked ourselves what we could do for them. We thought of trying to catch a char or a ptarmigan, but we hadn't had much luck lately. Then, in a flash of inspiration, Bernie envisioned a jelly doughnut.

We had become good doughnut cooks, but a jelly doughnut had seemed beyond our capabilities. We had a small amount of strawberry jam left. What remained was to get the jam inside the doughnut. Not a difficult problem by world standards, especially if you have a kitchen, but to us it posed a serious challenge.

Then Bernie's eye fell on the funnel used for transferring fuel from the gallon can to our small stove. It had a spout.

What could hold the jam? My sock. One with no more than two weeks' worth of wear in it. We pushed the funnel spout through the toe of the sock. We taped the sock to the lip of the funnel. What could be the plunger? We rummaged. The spoon? No. Not the right shape. The curry bottle!

With the apparatus assembled, all that remained was to see if it worked. Bernie readied the camera to record this moment of high-Arctic cuisine. I pushed the spout into the doughnut. I loaded the sock with jam. I readied the curry bottle. Had I majored in applied physics I might have foreseen what happened next. I gave the curry bottle a sharp jab. The doughnut exploded. Eventually we produced a dozen jelly doughnuts and wondered if the pilots would inquire how we got the jam into them. They never did. They eagerly ate their half on the flight home.

Later.　　A day doesn't pass without my hearing a rock-slide, but the trick is to see one. Like playing red light/green light as a kid, I wheel around when I hear one and look for movement. I rarely see where the ominous noise comes from.

Leaning over my fire this morning I heard one. Intent on not burning my pancakes, I didn't look up right away. The sound kept building. Sure that this would be one I could see, I looked. I scanned high up the opposite mountain. I could hear it, but still couldn't see it. I began to hear a rhythm. Looking lower, actually across the pond, I saw my rockslide: two caribou slogging through the shallows, knocking rocks around with their eight feet.

On yesterday's walk back to camp I did see one, backlit by afternoon light: a large, black boulder bouncing down a ridge, kicking up a spume of orange dust. I watched it bound downhill until it fell out of sight. I often pass house-sized boulders with open paths behind them. They appear to be alive, overgrown periwinkles or snails, moving slowly, stealthily downhill.

I see four distinct zones of mountainside: the highest, darkest, brooding peaks; the green swaths reaching up to points high on the mountainside, where alders, lichen, and grass act like glue to bind the rocks together; the second-oldest rock fields, where the lichen has just begun to grab hold; then the light, cream-colored areas of recent rockslides. The river's six ponds ahead of me have been caused by them. That's how narrow and steep the Palmer Valley is. I feel as though I'm walking in the bottom of a bowl with these few elements in the world: the mountains, the sky, and the line where they meet. There appears to be even less in the world when fog descends halfway to the valley floor and the massive mountain bases, which seem to be gathering themselves to shoot straight up forever, just end.

I was warned by Steve Loring, whose archaeological survey group traversed the valley last year, to camp where there's green. Then I'd know there hadn't been a recent rockslide.

I'd like to reach the first Palmer pond today. Gauging from the way the river looked yesterday, I should be able to. I'm allowing at least ten days to work my way up the valley to the watershed, or height of land. That seems a long time for only forty miles, but it's all uphill, and the way the crow flies isn't how I can walk.

My feet ache from walking over rocks in soft-soled shoes. I have two pairs, one pair of Chuck Taylor All-Star Specials (high-topped basketball sneakers) and one pair of L. L. Bean boots (rubber sole, leather top). I use the sneakers when I know I'll be in the water. I don't mind wet feet as long as I can put on dry socks at the end of the day. The canvas sneakers dry more quickly than leather. On my Bean boots the one thing I would change are the metal hooks on the boot uppers. They catch on twigs and branches. A pair with eyelets would have been better. A soft sole is better suited to canoeing than a hard sole, and I prefer the close contact with the earth they give me. Eventually my feet will toughen up, I hope.

Some *Outdoor Life* types express their relationship to nature aggressively. To them nature is a force to subdue, overcome, challenge, defeat, tame, or avoid. My irony is an inability to adopt that attitude, although I'm engaged in an activity that, in some people's minds, "pits" me against nature. But nature and I are not adversaries. My attitude is maternal, plantlike. My desire is to feel what's around me, to embrace it, to have it to nourish me, enter me. Why would I wish to contribute to an attitude that drives wedges between man and nature? It's misleading and clumsy to contribute to the further dissection of the world, a world in which all the events seem more now than ever to be mutually interdependent; an immense complexity of subtly balanced relationships.

I value firsthand experience and it's difficult for me to accept anything on faith without first putting it through my own little gristmill. I feel a part, a minuscule part, of something that began centuries ago. That something is to be part of the evolution of the verb "to explore." The verb has evolved from inspection to introspection, and, one hopes, is moving toward comprehension.

I remember an article that stated that the last three centuries have seen the discovery of every corner of the world. First the physical: explorers were inspecting the world, bringing it to our knowledge. Then in the last century began the microinspection of the world as exploration moved in multiple directions and disciplines of ever-more-minute investigations. Our century has seen the further transformation of the urge to explore along these multifarious angles of regard. It's been a process of fragmentation.

What excites me is to hope that as our century's obsession with self begins to wane, the new level of consciousness might initiate an attitudinal change in a worldwide way; that the predominant attitude of exploitation of nature will become inverted. I hope as an indication of our diminishing fear of the physical unknown that the world *with* becomes frequently substituted for *against* in people's minds when they think of themselves in relation to nature. It's the difference between the smug, man-centered world of a Jules Verne novel and the world-embracing attitude of Rimbaud's *The Drunken Boat*.

Evening.   The river is clear, so clear, and in most places shallow enough to walk in. It's all pebbles, rocks, and sand. The deepest parts are the outside curves, where the force of the current digs a deeper channel. Every time I come to one there's never an easy way around it. The willows hang out over the water, making it impossible to line past the deep spot from the bank. Often I portage, but sometimes I'm lazy and try to continue lining or bull my way through along the bank.

Almost lost *Monkey* today. Being lazy, trying to edge my way around a deep channel by crawling along the bank, my back to the willows, holding the canoe in tight, I tried pushing past a stiff branch. The bastard pushed back. Threw me into the river up to my hips. Holding onto *Monkey*, I slid downstream twenty yards before my feet touched bottom and I could get control. "With nature," indeed!

I'm very aware of the danger if I let the canoe's bow angle too far off the current. *Monkey* could swamp, sink, or break away from me. In my mind I've seen this happen a hundred times, a hundred different ways, with me standing helplessly in the river, watching it sweep downstream.

My day is in and out of water, moving from one side of the river to the other. I portage a dozen times. The shorter portages are more annoying than long ones because I am always putting something down and picking something up. I make four trips across each portage. I leave a distinct marker where I put down my first load. I take the canoe over last. The packs and wannigan would be easy to lose in the willows.

Question: "What happened to your food and gear?"

Answer: "Ahh, I lost them in the willows."

Over my first portages I'd make a point of walking a beeline between the beginning and the end. I thought if I broke my leg in the middle of a portage, they'd find me more easily, but now I realize I could break my back ten miles from camp or right in the tent; I'd still be in serious trouble.

Once I get used to the water temperature, I like walking knee-deep up the river. My eyes enjoy being close to the swirls and ripples of the current on the water surface. At the same time I feel the water's rush against my legs. I can see how the land tilts and forms the river, how the river forms itself around the land. It's very sexual. The river is the liquid surface of the earth following the land's contours in smooth, graceful movement. One problem I hadn't foreseen is how soft the water keeps my feet. This will cause me some painful blisters.

I'd thought I'd see some black bears by now. There are plenty of caribou, but no bears. Perhaps it's too early in the season for them to be in the Palmer Valley. Although I can see myriad patches of blueberries and cloudberries, there are no ripe ones. It's taken me these last five days to convince myself the odds are slim I'll be eaten by a bear. Often, these wacky boulders resemble them, or I think they do. Especially in the evening shadows, a slightly different-colored rock jutting up among its neighbors, a dark one caught sight of out of the corner of my eye, seems like a bear. Yesterday, on my walk to the pond, over my head in the willows, I couldn't see ten feet to either side. I heard a growl. My head jerked up. I bleated a loud "HELLO." Then felt stupid as my foot moved the rock again and the hollow, grating sound of rock on rock growled back.

Rather than building up, the weather arrives. This afternoon it became gray and ugly, especially down the valley around Nachvak Fiord. Then in late afternoon the sun broke through, blue sky took over. I portaged past a hectic cascade of a rapid and for the first time I was able to paddle upstream in the back-eddies. The river became wider. I could take a good, deep stroke. I was surprised to realize I was beyond the last rapid and into the V leading out of the pond — my goal.

Determined not to portage again, I left the back-eddy bent over the middle of *Monkey*, taking rapid strokes against the current, shouting at the top of my voice, "Salmon, salmon, trout, trout, jump up steeper drops than this."

Made it. Coasted into the pond. To my right was the small beach I had swum at the day before.

I've found a good campsite on a point, across from a water-fall, in the green away from rockslides. I'm pleased.

This slightly rounded pond is a calm break in the river's mad rush to the sea. I took *Monkey* out for a spin this evening. Everything seemed peaceful, level. The mountains looked majestic in the light. The pond was a smooth, flat surface. I tried opening *Monkey* up for speed by making a rhythm of long, deep strokes, then gliding. The small wave lines coming off the bow rolled away from the canoe in perfect symmetry. The cyclone swirls of my strokes, whooshing as I made them, dotted the water behind me as they unwound into smooth water again.

Then, I paddled without taking the blade out of the water. To do this I turn the handle in my palm as I finish the stroke, bring the blade forward edgewise, twist it, and sweep back in a normal stroke. The canoe moves forward, silent, a ghost.

Out on the pond, playing, I realized how full of concentration I've been. I felt a release throughout my body as the rhythm of paddling took over the need to watch where I was going. My head began to swivel like an owl's, looking right, left, not a care in the world. My body became one huge smile.

No fish yet, not even a rise, but it's a beautiful evening. I'm nestled on the point among the alders, by the fire, staying up to soak it all in.

The Torngats cry a lot, two types of tears: rocks and waterfalls. The tracks of the rockslides are the opposite of the waterfalls, they're the tracks of crying; the waterfalls are the living tears.

I can't get over the waterfalls. They come right off the

mountaintops, ragged white stripes dropping vertically hundreds of feet to disappear and reappear in their zigzag run down the mountainside. Their sound is strong wind in a forest or heavy breakers on rocks.

Sometimes in the daylight, the white water against the black rocks seems to be the white from the clouds pouring down to earth. Then in the semidarkness, the water glows whiter across the dark but not black shapes of the rocks. Always, they are white wonder, connecting heaven to earth.

How to acknowledge their power, their presence? The image of a waterfall. It's nonreproducible: no words, no painting, no photograph can convey its essence or substitute for being in its presence.

I know I'll try a hundred times. I've already made lots of sketches and some watercolors. At home, making a monoprint, I could use a stencil for the shape. The deckled edge of the torn paper could create the outside form of the fall. Using the stencil would block out the ink on the plate to complete the waterfall's form.

The colors: green, gray, orange, ochre, black: white vertical stripe traveling over multigraded mountain rock. How to abstract them? What I'd want to paint is the essence of the falls, not their surface look. It's a matter of not confusing what I see with what I'm doing on the canvas, but knowing them to be the same.

On an afternoon before I left home, I visited an art class being taught by the current czar of Boston art, Michael

A waterfall, Palmer Valley

Mazur. I listened to him discuss student work, then art in general and his eminently academic and lucid philosophy of it. He made it all sound very tidy, pre-Copernican. I envied him a little for being so sure about what art is because of my own confused and constantly shifting feelings about my own art. What I'm about is as mysterious and unknowable to me as this valley, these waterfalls. It escapes articulation or my rational comprehension. Always it's in my stomach, not my head, that I know I'm looking at good work or creating something good.

July 15.   The heat of the sun on the tent woke me. When it's out and there's no wind, the sun is hot, especially in the tent. An advantage to traveling alone is not being subject to another's bad dreams, snoring, rolling over, or personal time clock. On the other hand, no one's here to pull me up when I'm down, or to share the high points with.

I'm becoming aware of how much goes on inside my head. With people, I'm constantly distracted from listening to myself by interacting with them. Here, only while writing in the journal or making a watercolor do I feel more objective. Most of the time I am dreaming. I'm not constantly interrupting myself to someone, or cutting off a depth of thought, choosing to override a sight like the waterfalls by saying to a friend, "Isn't that beautiful."

There is a story about two Inuit brothers. One pitched his tent farther away from the river than the other. The anthropologist interviewing the former about how he kept in touch with his brother's feelings was told that "When I want to see how my brother is, I stand by my tent and wait to see him come out of his. I can tell how he is by watching him. Somehow, when I go up to him and we begin to talk, things become confused." Being silent is closer to being attentive.

There are definitely fish in the pond. I had oatmeal for breakfast, steel-cut oats. I washed out my pot, and minnows appeared. I'd love to catch a fish dinner.

Later. Canoe tied down three ways, paddles, too. Wind incredible. I'm sitting on the wannigan watching the storm build. No rain, yet. Wind warm, clouds thick and fast moving. . . .

I left camp after breakfast to walk up the side of the pond. Having seen minnows, I wanted to catch a fish. I tried and tried. I was using the spinning rod. It's my insurance. If I need to catch a fish, under some circumstances a Dardevle works better than a fly. Since I'd used my fly rod several times with no luck, I brought out the "meat ax," as Bernie used to call it.

On our trip, he never used it. He's too good and too pure a fly-fisherman. Only once did it create a friction between us. After a month on the Back River we'd become extremely efficient in dividing up our chores. At day's end, when the canoe touched shore, we unloaded. Then one of us set off to look for a tent site, set up the tent, and unroll the packs. The other found a place for the fire, built the fireplace, laid out dinner, and began collecting firewood. We grew uncomfortable with this system, but didn't say anything; we didn't realize our dissatisfaction arose because efficiency is only one level of teamwork.

One evening it was Bernie's turn to catch dinner. As always

he preferred the fly rod, but after an hour he returned empty-handed. I suggested using the spinning rod. The river was deep and had a heavy current. He didn't say anything. He went to try another spot.

No luck.

I went down to the river right in front of camp with the spinning rod, and two casts later had caught two large trout. The lure was able to sink deeper than the fly. It was as simple as that. Our frustration over our division of labor surfaced. We exploded. Talking it through we realized our efficiency was leading us farther away from each other. We were sharing less and less of camp life. After that we began working together, and this became a time-saver as well as allowing us not to lose touch with each other.

Our refound consideration for each other evolved into a simple set of words: "Would you like some tea?" Whether we had just finished tea, or were in the middle of a portage, or were about to be rained on, whenever one of us said, "Would you like some tea," we had tea. What we were really saying was, I'm so fucking tired or grumpy or thirsty that whatever *you* think, *I want to stop.* We always respected an invitation to tea and never asked more of each other until we'd had it.

Today, walking up the side of the pond, casting, the weather was fine and hot. There were no bugs. I reached an old rockslide of huge stones heaped in piles all the way into the pond. They had lots of quartz in them. I couldn't see the bottom. Because I was hot I took off my clothes, dove in. Ice cold. On the rocks drying, I was marveling at the lack of bugs as the first breeze of the day scuffled down the length of the pond. This was followed by another stronger one.

The sky was blue, pure blue. The light breeze became constant from the east. A premonition made me return to camp. I was thinking of my untethered canoe.

I've been back three hours. I've been watching the wind build and the clouds rumble by low overhead. I was going to make split-pea soup for dinner, but in this wind a fire would be hard to start. I'll have a bowl of granola and some cheese instead. The speed and multitude of clouds is like the scene in *The Wizard of Oz* where the witch's flying henchmen leave the castle to chase Dorothy's friends in the forest. Hordes of them blacken the sky. There is no escape. Eerie. That's how I feel.

Never seen such a variety of grays in a sky, such muscular, sinewy, circular, flexing, moving-head-over-heels clouds. They are flying over the mountaintops east to west. Occasionally, a tear in the clouds exposes blue sky. The clouds are a thin, sinister skin. Actually, they're beautiful, but I'm scared.

Now it's evening, or anyway dark, but not black. The clouds make it darker than it's been yet. The mountains have lost their form. They look flat in this dark light. The waterfall across from me glows. The wind plays with it, tossing it, making it undulate like a snake. I must be several miles from the top of the mountain and even farther from the waterfall, which is recessed into its own bowl. But I see it clearly. There's a lot of water tumbling down . . . I've stared so long, I'm seeing things. I see the mountain to the left of the fall as

A waterfall, Palmer Valley, night

the head of a giant bear resting his head on his paws, with his tongue out, the way a dog extends his on a hot summer day.

Now I'm really seeing things. Picked that waterfall right up, pushed it back over the top of the mountain. Great clouds of spume sucked up into the clouds. The wind picked the water up and held it there. Me riveted, mesmerized by hours of watching, then this! The wind pushed the water back up over the lip of the cliff.

Check the canoe. Tie it down one more way. What would the wind do to me and the tent? I move the tent deeper into the willows, into the hillside. Cut away some willows to make a tighter fit. Force myself to turn in. Try to sleep.

July 16.   Didn't sleep much. Concern about tent, wind, and gear. All night the wind beat on the tent. The storm was intense, as though I were inside a brown paper bag someone was crumpling. It was unnerving to see the wind stop the waterfall and push it effortlessly up into the sky.

In the middle of the night heavy rain woke me up. Went outside to check everything. Found *Monkey*'s stern two feet underwater. The pond had risen. I moved *Monkey* higher than the tent. Cursed all the work needed to untie my knots, then to retie them. Moved wannigan and baby. Before going in the tent, I stepped to the left into the willows to give one last look around. Noticed a small nest of twigs lined with white feathers. Empty. Hope I didn't drive them away by moving in.

Yes, I was afraid. My fear came right out and grinned at me. Made me realize just how fragile it is for me here.

By this morning, the combination of rain and wind pushing the water down the pond has raised the water level two more feet! Rain has stopped, but the wind is still high. Too high to move. I'll get a little of the sleep I missed.

Strong memory of Nick Shields. On the Eastmain River, near the beginning of the trip, going fishing — more to talk than to fish. Fog on the water so thick that we couldn't see anything. We talked about trusting ourselves enough to move into the unknown without fearing it. He knew some lines from Keats that go something like this: "To live in doubt and mystery without an irrational reaching after fact and reason."

Evening.   Wind up. Moved camp once again. Moved farther from the point, into the heart of the hill to get a solid rock wall and willow barrier between me and the wind. There's not much protection in the tundra. If the wind shifts, I shift. Hope this camp lasts. Moved *Monkey* and the wannigan. Tied *Monkey* down tight. Wouldn't want to lose the canoe. I'd look foolish saying, "My canoe blew away."

My respect only grows for the conditions here. At sunset, while I had the pressure cooker building up a good head of steam, the sun came out to illuminate a receding-down-the-valley squall, creating the first arc of rainbow I've seen. I took several photographs of it. The light was all on my side of the rainbow. Beyond it were dramatic black clouds, small streaks of cerulean blue under them and a stark white waterfall off to the left. The lower valley looked dark and ominous. No Hudson River School painter could have asked for more. The rainbow, like that small bird singing, filled the valley with its beauty. I watched it move down the valley, drifting along above the river, an arc whose curve accentuates the cragginess and steep pitch of the mountains to either side.

The stove works like a charm. I made pea soup from dry split peas in about half an hour. None of this powdered, plastic hooey food where the servings are minimal and the taste good mainly because I'm hungry. Having the pressure cooker makes it possible to eat handsomely.

I cut several slices of bacon, with lots of fat, and fried them in the bottom of the cooker. Then I added water and the peas, built up a head of steam, pushed the valve down, and cooked it for twenty minutes under pressure. I removed it from the fire, allowing the steam to ease on its own, not by snapping up the valve. This adds about ten extra minutes but makes all the difference. Having patience for the last step is the hardest, especially if I'm hungry, but it's still cooking while it cools.

The alfalfa seeds are sprouting. Salad with dinner in about a week. I'd never found the ideal container for sprouting seeds until this summer. I needed something lightweight, clear, and with a porous top. At Denny's appeared the perfect item: one of his daughter's baby bottles. Besides meeting every requirement, it's the right size for a one-man salad. By replacing the nipple with a piece of cheesecloth, the seeds can be rinsed, drained, and aired. If the weather is cool I can carry the bottle in my pocket, or keep it with me in the sleeping bag at night.

I knew the perfect weather of the first five days couldn't last. Now I've tasted some mean weather. As I climb higher into more exposed territory I'll have to pick camp carefully. In fact, two camps, one for reserve in case the weather changes.

The sun is lost behind the mountains. The valley is a gray wash. The wind is still high. Eerie, all this space, just me, the rocks, and the roar of the wind. I have to keep telling myself that most of the noise is from the waterfalls, not the wind. I can tell which side of the valley the wind favors by which waterfall carries the louder sound. Cool night.

July 17.   Awful night. I stayed half awake waiting for the tent poles to buckle or to hear the *bang-bang-bang* of the canoe blowing away. Rain half the night. Now fog, cold, and wet. Ugh. A Northeaster.

Snowed last night. Not where I am but high up the mountainside. It's as though a horizontal climate-change line was drawn on the mountains. The top third of the mountains is covered in fresh snow. The white is cut open by black rocks poking through. An ugly sky breathes down above the peaks. Uninviting. I'm not moving today. Back to bed.

I've been here a week and barely traveled twelve miles. I have several more days before reaching "the Porch," the watershed. It's a good thing I've five long weeks to reach the island where I'll meet Richard. I'm not rushing. I've never gone on a trip just to "get it done." In other accounts of canoe trips, it often appears that part of the quality of the trip is based on how fast it's accomplished. That seems a contradiction to me. I've always enjoyed making them last as long as possible.

Evening.   I did something I still can't believe the afternoon I reached this pond. After setting up camp on the point,

I went fishing. There wasn't much breeze. I set up the spin-ning rod and trolled. I wanted to scout ahead and this was a good way to do it. There are two sections to the pond. Where they meet the water becomes shallower, the current stronger. Great place for fish.

Passing over a submerged boulder, but feeling lazy, I didn't reel in. Sure enough, I snagged the boulder. This was the first time I'd used the spinning rod. I hadn't set the drag. The line broke. Mad at myself, I paddled back to see if I could spot the lure. Glinting in the sunlight, the lure was dangling off the edge of the rock. I didn't have extra lures that I could afford to lose.

Holding *Monkey* in position in the current, I climbed out on the boulder a hundred yards from shore, up to my crotch in water. One hand held the canoe, the other went under-water. Even my head went under in order to reach the lure. What I don't remember is how I got back in the canoe. Lure in hand, I must have swung my leg up and jumped in. I just don't remember. Thinking back on it, I shudder. It was dumb.

July 18.   Good weather! Had a head wind paddling up the pond, but no problem handling *Monkey*. Being alone, I work harder. With two people paddling, one can catch his breath while the other continues to paddle.

If the canoe is loaded with more weight toward the bow, the wind has a harder time blowing it off course. If I had a tail wind, I'd want some extra weight in the stern.

Made a long portage between the first two ponds. To go down to the river to line for fifty yards just to portage again didn't make sense. The portage was a mile long. The mountainsides are terraced. There are no alders, lots of grass and moss. I had to go up a steep incline, then down one, then up the next. On top of the terrace the walking is easy as long as I stay out of the wet spots.

I have trouble keeping my footing on wet rocks. I can usually tell if the rock is wet, but sometimes there is a thin, loose layer of moss on top. When my weight goes on the moss, especially if it is on an incline, down I go. That can hurt with eighty pounds on my back.

Began the day thinking I'd line up between the ponds. Where the river comes into the first pond, I changed into my sneakers, got out the bow and stern lines, and started walking upstream. Cold. The river was still high from the rain. The water was too deep to walk against. It had flooded into the willows, making lining along the bank impossible.

As I started walking in the water, I saw an unusual light color just under the surface. A peculiar color to see when everything is a combination of the same basic earth tones. A light flesh color stands out. Before I realized what it was, I had picked it up. A baby bird so small its eyes hadn't opened. There were no feathers on its body; the cream color of its flesh was what caught my eye. The beak and stomach were much larger than its scrawny neck and tiny wings. The rain must have washed it out of its nest.

I portage where the going looks easier, along the right side of the river. I had hoped to carry only two loads on each portage. Instead I carry four. That means seven trips over each portage. I could double up two loads, but bending down to put the second load on top of the first is impossible. Perhaps when I've eaten some food and lessened the baby's weight I can. I walk slowly. There is plenty of time. I've no schedule to keep. If it takes all day, it takes all day. I tend to wander high uphill if I'm with my thoughts, my eyes on the ground directly in front of me. To be fully attentive to what I do as I do it, that is the goal.

In the forest, I follow a trail when I portage. If the trail is hard to see I look for blazes and follow them. Here I follow my nose. The game trails are made by the caribou. As much as I like the caribou, I don't trust them, at least not as trail-blazers. I never know where they're going to lead me. Often, their trails are good indicators of the various choices. They can indicate the driest, easiest route, but often they don't. Where they go and where I want to go are usually different . . . so I follow my nose.

Carrying my first load, skirting the edge of a swampy patch, I flush a ptarmigan. She flies up in front of my feet. Instead of playing the decoy she keeps right on flying. Un-usual. I bend to look where she's flown from and find her nest. In it are seven tan eggs with deep brown speckles. That is why she waited so long before bolting. When their chicks are young, the adults stay close to the danger, running or fly-hopping along the ground just out of reach. They are trying to draw the enemy away from their brood. At other times they hide, statuelike, trusting their camouflage more than they should. It's as if they close their eyes and pretend I don't see them. Often when they do this I can walk right up to them. Both these reasons make them easy prey for a man with a gun or a good throwing arm.

Over the rest of the portage I think about eggs: eggs in omelettes, quiche, cakes, bread, pastry, cookies, mayonnaise, hollandaise, eggs over easy, sunny-side up, poached, shirred, painted, hardboiled, raw, scrambled, broken. What doesn't have eggs in it? What culture doesn't depend on them as a staple? Eggs: universal, mysterious, versatile, full, life, the earth, round, curves, fundamental, moon, woman, the perfect package, Fabergé . . . eggs.

With each load I cross a stream, taking several steps into bubbling white water where I can't see my feet. I try not putting my full weight down until I know the water's depth and whether the foothold is stable. The extra weight on my back adds stability to me in the current. The stream tumbles down out of the mountain following its north-south course. Its left bank, steeper and shadier, retains patches of snow. It's the first snow I've walked on since the first day in the fiord.

Looking over a distance, the landscape tends to flatten itself out. The white patches of snow appear to be on the same plane as the protruding rocks. It's my mind, not my eyes, that tells me the snow is in the deepest gullies, in the shadiest spots. Like looking at the ocean from a distance, if I look with my eyes, not my mind, the water appears more like a wall than a flat surface. The Chinese perceive the landscape with their eyes and they paint with their mind in their hands. Their landscape paintings puzzled me at first because they seemed flat.

The wind was stronger bringing the canoe over. It gusted off the pond up the hill I had to climb down. Every few steps I'd have to stand still, feet apart, body braced to keep from blowing sideways. I'm a funny sight walking with a fourteen-and-a-half-foot oblong shape on my head. I can imagine the snide remark a female caribou could make.

≈

There are all shapes and sizes of driftwood piled up at this end of the second pond. More firewood than I have seen. Some pieces thick as my forearm, not just the thumb-sized ones I usually find. I took a few of the larger pieces with me in the canoe.

Although I wanted to be at the head of the second pond, I looked for campsites along the way. This pond is larger than the first. It's a thin, mile-long slit in the valley. It's several hundred yards wide. The wind drifted me sideways. The waves were a foot and a half high. This gave me the chance to test *Monkey* under these conditions.

As the wave sets flow down at me, I try and have the bow meet them at a slight angle. This way the canoe passes over them without slapping the water and remains steadier. At the head of the pond the mountain drops, *bam*, into the water. Coming down from the third pond, the Palmer is one big rapid.

Between the two ponds the wind is blocked out by a solid wall of willows. I made camp to the left of where the river comes in, right near several large bear scats. I'm sure we both wish to avoid each other, but in case he likes bacon more than his privacy, I put the food where I can watch it. I have two antibear weapons. One is my cast-iron frying pan, the other is a cherry bomb. If banging on the pan doesn't scare him away, the firecracker going off beside him will. I hope.

I was in New York last springtime and went to the Central Park Zoo to see the bears. Although the odds were slim I'd meet one on my trip, I wanted to see what I'd be up against if I did. They cage two polar bears beside two grizzly bears. Their cages aren't big.

Considering a polar bear thinks nothing of ranging hundreds of miles through the Arctic in search of food, their life in the park looked miserable. Their two neighbors, Hiawatha and Pocahontas, the grizzlies, certainly thought it was. They paced neurotically, continuously, back and forth the width of their cage, to turn quickly by swiveling on their hind feet, never stopping, a perpetual motion.

The polar bears seemed more accepting of their fate. At least they did the day I stood there looking through the bars. One of them lay on his side, almost with an air of indifference, as if to say, "Well, it could be worse. Plenty of people in this city have harder lives and pay more for them than I do." The other bear was playing. He'd slide down a shoot into a pool of water over his head. He'd stay underwater blowing bubbles! Sometimes he'd surface face first, more often feet first.

Their playfulness allowed me to think running into a polar bear might not be so bad . . . and reminded me of my Aunt Edith, who tells a Thanksgiving story called "The Preacher and the Bear." Preacher is cornered by bear and falls to his knees to pray. Bear follows suit. The preacher thinks he's made a convert and congratulates the bear. The bear remarks, "I'm not praying, I'm saying grace."

The other thing I saw, which I had never noticed before, was a barometer. After seeing the bears, I walked through the park and past the Plaza Hotel. Mounted on one of the pillars at the front entrance was a handsome French barometer. I liked the idea that anyone passing could consult a barometer and see what the weather would be doing.

The sun has gone behind the mountain rim. Again, I watch that strong, harsh line of shadow creep up the mountain, leaving me in shadow. It's still early afternoon. Overhead, the sky is blue, the clouds are white.

I've brewed a cup of tea. I am sitting by the fire sipping it. Across from me is a beautiful, white-falling-cream of a water-fall. Because of the strong wind, the water sound is blown away from me. I can't hear it, which makes it seem like a silent movie.

Nature: small elements standing in contrast to larger ones, standing in contrast to even larger ones. Each one joining the others to contribute to an overall relationship.

Space: the empty space, the air in the valley is as real as the rocks. Never felt that before. I had always looked through space to something. Not here.

Scale: the tundra on the Back River was unsettling because what seemed far was near, what seemed large was small. Here it's reversed. The distance my eye travels is up and down, not across and out. What seems close at hand is far away, what seems small is huge.

Horizon: I'm used to having a horizon line to relate to. The tundra implies flatness. It's another type of horizon in a deep valley like this. A strange sensation I like a lot. After all, a horizon is only the limit to what I can see.

The mountains are an embarrassment to me. No, rather my inability to make a powerful watercolor of them is an embar-rassment. However, the waterfalls, the mountains, the lichen, and all their colors are entering me. They'll come back out when they're ready. There is one lichen, a screaming orange one, I never get used to. It's the loudest color here. It stands out among all the gray, green, and black lichens.

I'm not satisfied with the watercolors. They're terrible. No drama, no character.

I took out the thumb piano tonight. I played and played and played. I was depressed when I began. I was in a terrible mood. I played on and on and on, giving as much thought to the silence between the notes as to striking new ones. My mood soared as the sound ordered the space around me and in me. The thumb piano is a hollow box shape with seventeen metal fingers, or keys. The notes are made with the thumbs while I hold the box. It's small enough to bring and a great pleasure to play.

There must be fish in this pond, but if there are, they must be invisible. Nothing. The evening has become calm. There's a hatch on, but nothing is rising. The water is dark. Over it float hundreds of white wings. They rise and fall, hit the water surface, making little rings. It's just what a hungry trout or char would want. Tomorrow I'm going to do some punchy, direct watercolors . . . and catch a fish.

July 19.   Several of the watercolors aren't so bad, but none of them really sings. That depresses me. Go for a walk.

Painting: start with a feeling, a desire, start to work. Make the first few lines or put down a color combination. Choose to leave it or not. Work over it. Lose it. Find it. Lose it. Find it again. Stop. What I want to see is what I haven't seen. Obliterate what I have and start again. Lazy, I stop. The following day it says, "You stopped too soon." One day I'll stop with something I don't like. The next morning it looks great. The courage to stop when it's right, the courage to go beyond what looks good. How to proceed.

The third pond is right around the corner. One short portage over a rockslide. The rockslide is full of blooming or about to bloom river beauties, a robust pink flower of the tundra. They stand out strongly; their leaves and stalks are a chalky green. One group is growing in front of a black rock. I'll go back and paint that boldly, clearly. But I was . . .

Thunder.

Just had time to cover everything before the rain. That thunder cracked and my stomach contracted. The voice of the Torngat.

The river beauty is one of those fragile, fundamental elements of the tundra, like the baby bird or the ptarmigan eggs, that stands in sheer contrast to the solidity and massiveness of the rocks, the mountains. It is related to the fireweed, the coarse, tall purple weed growing in marshy places along roadsides at home. This northern cousin has adjusted to its harsher conditions, and grows low to the ground. Unlike fireweed, it's a delicate flower that bobs and bounces in the wind. It doesn't try to stand up to it. Walking through half an acre of them, I felt I could almost hear them singing.

Over breakfast I was thinking about my family. I grew up in a home where the expression of deep inner feeling was taboo. Everybody treated everyone else formally, in a very New England, very WASP way. The seven of us, my three sisters, my brother and I, and my parents, were supposed to control our emotions. What I was supposed to do with them no one ever said. If I was awkward enough to show them, I was made to feel guilty. Arguments between my parents rarely surfaced in front of us. This was how they had been raised. This was how we'd be raised. Silence was enough to express disapproval. It was effective, and repressive.

If I don't attempt to resolve those qualities I dislike, or break the bad habits I grew up with, I'll pass them right along to my children. An aspect of the conflict is the amount of time I've spent as an emotional stowaway: I muffle, cloud, and avoid emotions I don't want to face. Inside one black steamer trunk stowed inside me is the thought that my folks couldn't pass on to me something they hadn't received, or achieved, for themselves.

My whole being is directed toward expressing my feelings, or trying to. I'll be breaking a long habit if I begin to do that. As a college freshman in 1967, what challenged me was the implied goal of my life to "make it" better than the Old Man. The idea seemed to be to put off what I might like to do, or intuitively was drawn to do. The message was to put it off until, say, "later" when I'd served my time. Then I'd be free to pursue what I wanted. The problem was that I had no idea what "making it" meant. However, right then, at eighteen, I knew I wanted to pop one of those little orange zowies right in my mouth. And I did.

Drugs were supposed to expand my horizons, alter my perceptions, deepen them. The desire for change was a real one, but might have been better answered by posing a question about what was wrong with me as I was that I needed to alter my perceptions with that there little pill.

They'd never harp on it, but my folks want me to settle down, get married, have children, and pursue a career with a social and economic security they understand.

My father's refusal to be moved by what moves me, and his disappointment that I'd make canoeing and painting my life, tend to push me more toward those things, not away from them. I wonder if he'd understand that the waterfalls I live with here, the sight of all those river beauties today, mean to me exactly what a well-kept house, a good investment, or a photograph of the boat on the mantel mean to him: a sign of order in chaos, the rewards of persevering along your own

lines. That his chaos happens to be my element is not important.

Evening. For dinner tonight we're featuring rice with
ramen and tamari, several slices of bacon, topped off by my
first alfalfa-seed salad, cooked and served in the tent due to
inclement weather.

Several challenges arise in preparing a meal inside the tent.
The first being not to burn the tent down while cooking the
meal. The wooden wannigan top, with a pot top underneath
the stove, keeps the heat from melting the tent floor. Starting
the stove with a pot on top of it helps keep exuberant flames
off the tent walls. The second challenge is serving the meal. I
have a wooden bowl I eat from (being wooden, it can hold a
hot meal or liquid without burning me). Putting *Salade de
la Maison* on top of the *Reis mit Speck* and eating a careful
stratigraphy, the separation of courses is maintained with a
minimum of dirty dishes.

For dessert, tea and a piece of candied ginger. Sharp tastes
are welcome and candied ginger is a good one. I can cook
with it, too. It shapes up a curry meal. Eating ginger straight
wakes up the taste buds, or cut up and added to rice dishes it
gives a backbone to the other spices. It and the sourballs are
the candy I brought. On the Back River, Bernie and I
thought having gum would be good. The idea was that it
wouldn't disappear right away. We brought lots of Double-
Bubble and grew to hate it, but we could never bring ourselves to throw it away, either. Tabasco sauce is another
strong, welcome taste.

I tend to eat fast, especially in the woods when I'm hungry.
With other people meals are a social time, conversation nat-

urally lengthening meals. By myself food could disappear quickly, but I eat with chopsticks. I've realized it's no less a social time for me. My thoughts are plenty of company.

The first days out I was looking up the valley at the snow-fields on top of the mountains ahead. Now that I'm under them I look back and see the snow on the ones I was under before. I'm under the most ominous black crags now. I look back at the lighter-colored ones. They have a strong, muscular quality. After a rain, they glisten like a sweating body. With the sun out after a rain, chips of white light dot the landscape. This is the sun reflected off wet rocks, which act like a mirror.

I've gained considerable elevation in the last two days. I feel as though I'm actually on a mountain, not in a valley. The Torngats rise straight up from sea level to staggering heights of several thousand feet: different from New England mountains, like Mt. Washington, that begin at least several hundred feet above sea level. The mountains here are full of crazy lines. Great shifts of rock, caused when they were born, mark lines of seemingly haphazard movement. Perched on top of their talus slopes, the peaks look like wacky millinery mobiles. The ridges thrown in sharp relief against the sky are broken by the humps of individual boulders. The boulders appear to be sitting elevated on the ridges as though they chose their vantage points to gain better views.

There's a process of smoothing occurring here. The acres of stone fields stretching away from me are made up of different types of rocks. Some are angular, others smooth. The ones near the river or waterfalls are made smooth by the washing of many waters. The other rocks retain their sharp corners.

Gray is a favorite color among them. It acts as a strong color, not the neutral tone I usually think of.

I've traveled ten days without bugs; seven of the ten have been good weather, usually cool with clouds. T-shirt weather in the sun. I expected worse. This side of Hudson Bay is notorious for its bad weather and rain. If the weather mirrors the landscape it will be full of strong contrasts.

No fish. After the first squall, I took *Monkey* on the flat-calm pond, determined to catch a fish. I trolled a streamer slowly, I trolled fast. I changed to a dry fly that matched the white moths and cast into corners. I let the canoe glide while I looked for movement against the bottom of the pond. There are small white moths, hundreds of them, on the water and a hatch of small brown insects. If there were a rise, I'd see it. Nothing. I wonder what the reason is? Either I'm not being perceptive enough or there are no fish. The beauty of fishing is the ability to transform line, metal, and feather into believable, living movement. The last refinement is the fisherman's ability to live at the end of the hook, to live with it as it moves through the water. People who fish, really fish, can do this. I've been doing some drawings of fish — if I can't catch them, I can draw them.

Exquisite within all the silence here is the reflection of the sky and mountains in the pond's mirror surface. The water is clear and shallow enough so that the rocks beneath the surface seem to be in the sky. Watching this reminds me of what Henry David Thoreau used to do to increase his perceptions: he'd bend over and look at the landscape through his legs.

Last May on my visit to New York when I saw the bears, I went with Willard Trask for my first visit to the Pierpont Morgan Library. Willard is a translator and author with a passion for the box that Thoreau made to house his journals. He'd intended to see it for the last thirty years. They never show it. He never bothered to push it. Thoreau had built it to house his notebooks; now the library houses the box. Because of my job at the Boston Athenaeum I thought I could smooth the way. We were admitted, but the librarian was suspicious of our request. She kept asking if we didn't mean the journals themselves. No, we insisted on the box. Still skeptical, she allowed us to be taken into the vault to see the box. It's a simple three-foot oblong pine box with brass fittings. The interesting aspect is that Thoreau built it so a side opens, making the box a portable shelf. The journals' spines face out. Its used and battered appearance glowed in its pristine surroundings. To hear it calling to be touched, used again, handled, moved, made me sad.

A curious experience occurred during that same day. I was staying with Annie Loui on South Eleventh Street in Williamsburg, Brooklyn. She's a mime just beginning to establish herself in New York. She lives in a loft in an old mustard-colored factory a block back from the East River. She has a knockout view of Manhattan, but it's a poor neighborhood, part Hispanic and part Hassidic Jews. The Hassidic Jews in their long black coats and black hats are the opposite of the Hispanics, who appear as colorful birds of paradise. Like the tundra, it's a community of sharp contrasts.

Leaving Willard, I came out of the subway at Marcy Avenue to see the weather had deteriorated to cold wind and rain. Gray clouds the color of concrete pressed down on the city. I was hurrying back to Annie's, head down and body bent into the rain. The black, punched-out windows, the abandoned buildings along Division Avenue reflected the day's bleakness. The only glistening things were the hundreds of bottle caps squashed into the tar. Hugging a wall, I came to the corner of Division and Driggs avenues. At the same time, from the opposite right angle, came a group of Hassidim. We met face to face at the corner of the building. I could have knocked the lead man down. I jumped back. I crossed the street. I stood watching the procession pass.

Six men struggled under the weight of a clear pine box on their shoulders. A black cloth was draped over it. A coffin. There were no handles and they struggled not to drop it. I had almost plowed right into them. I shuddered to think of the *New York Post*'s headline: BOSTON WASP STOMPED TO DEATH BY HASSIDIM. I thought of the box Willard and I had seen that afternoon in the Morgan Library, itself resembling a coffin in its surroundings. I thought about New York, where such diverse events happen in a day. In that ant-heap city, one is formed by men, not by nature. I saw people all that day who had been ground, frayed, polished, and shaped, or misshaped, by constant contact with each other, like stones in a turbulent river.

At dinner, tonight, I opened David Bosworth's second envelope:

> We are to have what we have as if it were loaned to us and not given; to be without proprietary rights to body or soul, mind or faculties, worldly goods or honors, friends, relations, houses, castles, or anything else.
>
> Possessions: you possess only whatever will not be lost in a shipwreck.

July 20.   Rained a lot last night. I stayed awake loving to hear the rain on the tent, knowing I wasn't going to get wet.

At times, the rain sound was thick enough to drown out the even louder sound of the nearest waterfall. Finally, the rain ended. A strong wind persisted. I drifted off to sleep to the sound of wind playing with the waterfall sound. The wind brought the sound closer to me, then would push it farther away.

Then — *bang!* Awake. Sweating. Terrified: the floating water sound mixing with sleep became confused with voices. I couldn't breathe. Sleeping bag tight around me, gripping me. Packs!

Caught in a halfway world where I snapped awake from something I felt, or dreamed I felt, I relived entering the mental hospital.

The sleeping bag's mummy shape held me. I was in packs strapped on a long worktable in the white-tiled shower room of Bowditch Hall. Packs are a crude restraining technique, a simple and sinister method of "protecting you from yourself." Uncomprehending, I was wrapped mummylike in damp sheets until only my head showed. Scream, kick, writhe, I couldn't break that cocoon. I blacked out.

I lay there sweating, remembering the feeling of packs from eleven years ago. A kaleidoscope of memories kept me awake.

April of my first year at college. Around my birthday, not eating or sleeping for three days. Walking all night in the city, along highways, over bridges, resting at the side of the road curled up like an animal. See into people, all their fears, their worries, their good qualities, their feelings. Tell them what I see, everything. Everything becoming an association, one huge association, me not discriminating between my inside world and the outside one. I lost my boundaries. Pulled in a thousand directions, filled with a thousand different feelings, I became a cup for the world. Not one feeling my own, not one of them lasting. I was on one huge slide into a confused, desperate consciousness. The only constant in my world being the speed at which I changed.

Information: I wanted to be taken care of. I walked forty miles from Cambridge to Manchester, Massachusetts, to my parents' house. It was a trick getting over the Mystic River Bridge without being stopped. I arrived near dawn. The house was locked. I sat on the porch. My parents were asleep. The house seemed to be a huge cat. I could hear it purring. I sat on the porch. I stared at the sky. The soft spring breeze felt good. The moon behind the clouds transformed them into human images: sections of bodies, arms, legs, torsos, men, women all tumbled in pieces across heaven. All I could hear in my head was a voice saying, "You've lost your keys. You've lost your keys." I was scared.

My parents woke up at their usual time. They were surprised to see me. I had nothing to say, but expected them to know what I wanted. My father went to work. My mother was worried. She told me to go lie down. I lay down. I got up and pulled the shades. I lay down again. I got up. I couldn't sleep. There was too much in my head. There was too much to do, but what exactly was it? I followed my mother around the house, silent. She didn't know what to do or say. I left.

I walked back to Cambridge. I passed a lawn with a wire strung at knee level to keep people off the new grass. The wire began vibrating. I had made it move by looking at it. I had entered another world.

What to do?

Return to the boarding school I had gone to, an hour's ride from Cambridge. Even put on a coat and tie to look presentable. Ride the subway out there. Hear the same words, "You've lost your keys," but this time it seems everyone on the subway is saying it to me. Go to the minister's house. Meet his wife at the door, garden trowel in her hand. Welcomed in. She goes to find her husband.

Why am I here?

I sit waiting.

I read the paper.

I watch all the black-and-white words become black-and-white letters become black-and-white shapes become black-and-white chaos become . . .

"Hello, Mr. Cleveland. Thought I'd . . . thought I'd come say hello because I am Cleaving-land, leaving Cleveland, because . . ."

He kept me quiet, tried to feed me, to get me to talk about what happened, get me to sleep. Bathe. Into the spare bed in the study. Up an hour later. House silent, sleeping, me in his study. Open a filing cabinet. Read a few sermons. Disagree with a few things. Begin to correct his prose. Add a few paragraphs of my own. So what if they spill over his desk, onto the walls. Everything becomes my paper. Put the clock in a drawer. I can still hear it. It is the sound of a kitten lapping milk. Work until dawn. Put in my eight hours. There's the phone. Call home. The Old Man answers. Tell him how, when the sun wakes up, so does his son. "Where are you?" Tell him. Then wake up the Clevelands. Better yet, get in bed with them. Mr. Cleveland bolts up. All I wanted was to be taken care of. Go downstairs, wait in the kitchen. Wait in the kitchen. Wait. Terrified. Of what? Just terrified . . .

My father took me to the college infirmary. Until then I

felt everything was going to work out, but once there I began to realize maybe things weren't.

Lying in the infirmary bed I hear the same sound I heard last night, the sound that woke me — a susurrus of voices outside my room. The voices are telling me I have a chance to prove I am all right. This is a birthday rite all nineteen-year-olds pass through. It's perfectly normal. Out in the hall are my friends, my parents, the doctor. They are whispering. What they want me to do is to get out of bed, walk out in the hall, and say, "Hi, I'm fine." They'll say, "Happy birthday."

I'll do them one better and go out in my birthday suit. I have on white hospital pajamas, the cotton ones with the pullover top and the drawstring around the waist. I take them off, walk into the hall. Surprise! No one there I know. Two uniformed guards sitting either side of the door. They are nervous, not knowing what kind of a wacko I am.

The guard on the left, a short black man, gets up, turns me around, leads me back into the room. He starts helping me put on the pajamas. He holds the pants, I step in. He ties the string around my waist. He slips the top over my arms. I lower my arms on his shoulders. Being much shorter than me, he's nervous. He pulls away. Even more nervous than he is, I hold on to him. We fall. We roll under the bed. We upset the bed, him yelling "Murder," me not understanding. Confusion.

Several large, earnest men appear. They hold me down. A nurse comes in, gives me two shots of Thorazine in the ass. I'm on my way to the maximum-security ward of the mental hospital in a straightjacket, strapped to a cot, carried in an ambulance, for having attacked a black man. I was what they call a "live one."

I wake up on a bare mattress in a blue, bare room. There is one screened window opposite a door with no door handle. A small vertical rectangle of window is cut in the door. I have no idea where I am, how I arrived, or what's going to happen next.

I feel I've been out that way a long time. I know in the dusty way you feel things waking up from a dream that there is a game of horseshoes being played outside the window. I can hear the heavy clunk in the sand, and once in a while the clang of metal on metal. On the other side of the room at the little window, a man's face appears, stays a moment, disappears.

I lie perfectly still. Something tremendous has happened. To me? What is it? Scattered images, sensations rush through me unedited, uncut-and-all-at-once.

I wake again. A woman is talking. To me? She is kneeling on the floor by my mattress. A man stands watching. She holds a white something in each hand. What is she saying? She touches me. I don't dare move. They leave.

Several men come into the room. They hold me, pull down my pants. Fight and scream. I can't stop the woman who holds the needle, can't stop her from giving me the shot. I feel burning heat in my ass and black out. This sequence repeats itself, often.

It took months to understand I was on a hall called Bow-ditch, a hall named after the famous New England navigator. That it was the maximum-security ward at McLean Hospital. That I had had what was described as a nervous breakdown. That if I did not take my medication orally, I'd get it in the ass. That the sooner I behaved responsibly, the sooner I would get well. That I would remain in this prison as long as I acted up. That privileges came to those who could handle them. Everything was a privilege, from going to the bath-room alone, to carrying a lighter, to eating with silverware instead of plastic spoons, forks, and knives, to spending half an hour walking in the backyard alone. Everything was a privilege to be worked for. Everything. And they could be taken away instantly, not always for just cause.

I learned it was three weeks between the time I entered and the day I connected the sound of horseshoes with their name. Those first three weeks are a jumble of sensations, shots, packs, tears, and terror: unconcious of where I was, what was happening, what it meant. My thread of meaning had snapped.

I learned to smile a lot, even if I didn't mean it. If I disliked authority before, the complete subjection of that year made me grow to hate it. On the positive side, I developed a deep appreciation for the pleasure of being alive, the few simple things allowed to me, the ordinary activities of the day. I developed a strong belief in the individual as more fundamental than any larger group, like society. Not the isolated person, but the individual as the fundamental building block, instead of special-interest groups. It seems in an age of group pressure, global responsibility, that the individual has less and less power over his destiny, but it seems the farther from the individual the decision-making process removes itself, the more often logical decisions are made without any trace of human feeling.

That year I had little control. The nurses, the doctors, the aides controlled me. I heard authority every time an aide pulled out his keys, which was most of the time, since everything was locked. There were three locked doors to go through to get outside.

Some aides became friends, but it took only one bad aide to make patients miserable.

Bill had it in for me, as well as for everyone else. He'd

enter my personal space, put his mug four inches away from mine, waiting for me to fidget, react. If I did, he'd question me, "What's wrong, Rob? You seem uncomfortable. Wouldn't you like to tell me about it?" If I belted him in the face, I'd be in trouble. If I told him to fuck off, I'd be written up in the nurses' book as exhibiting aggression. Best defuse myself and smile.

One memory: the hall couch was down twenty feet from the kitchen door. I was sitting on the couch. Bill came out of the kitchen, coffee in hand, key in the door. He turned to push the door shut with his foot as a patient came up to ask him for a cup of coffee. Patients weren't allowed into the kitchen by themselves. Aides were supposed to help them if the kitchen was open. Bill looked straight at the patient as his foot nudged the door shut, and said, "No, sorry, as you can see the kitchen is closed." The patient went rigid. Bill waited, relaxed, sipping his coffee, to see what would happen. Nothing would've pleased him more than to get a violent reaction. Nothing happened. The patient walked off. I could've done something, said something, but I remained paralyzed, afraid to jeopardize my privileges.

Several months later, in the fall, Bill got his. A privilege granted me was to saw and split wood several afternoons a week. It became an obsession. One the doctor approved of, as it made me happy and put wood in his cellar. I'd go with an aide into the small woods behind the hall. Once Bill came with me to supervise. It's boring watching someone else work. He walked around some. He sat down and watched. He picked a twig off a bush next to him and chewed it. Before we left he'd chewed another twig off the same poison sumac. For the next two weeks he was out of work with a severe rash on his lips, in his mouth, and down his throat. It wasn't very generous on my part not to ask him if he knew what he was chewing.

I turned a corner toward getting out when an older patient, named Correll, arrived on the hall. When new patients came they usually arrived at night and were there the next morning, like Christmas. He had only one leg. The other he had recently lost to cancer. He was a cancer researcher at M.I.T., and when he wound up analyzing the cancer in his own stump, he went crazy.

He became the "looka-busy" man for me. He relit my enthusiasm. The first time he caught me by surprise by asking me to make his bed. You're supposed to make your own. Most patients just threw the sheets over the cot, but being in a wheelchair, he had a hard time maneuvering around the bed. I said I'd make it for him. Sure. I went in his room and threw it together. He looked at it and remarked that he didn't think it was well made. I spent the better part of the morning working on that bed, and didn't mind.

Then he asked me if I knew what the Greek alphabet was. No. He said, well, this is Omega, and he drew it on a napkin for me. He said if I wanted to know the others he'd teach them to me. And I did.

I used to show him my drawings and watercolors, looking for his praise. He'd tell me they were terrible (which they were). That only made me mad to do more.

I had always liked to draw, but considered it the province of my sisters. In the hospital I began to draw and paint watercolors intensely. No technical virtuoso, this kid, but each piece of work was, in some way, an exercise of my freedom. I felt that in my stomach. Those first ones are full of a confused energy, but then as now each one opens a process into myself, to the part of me ordinarily hidden and repressed. I go to a place beyond the day to day (even if the subject is not), a place always more potential than realized. Yet, a place no one knows better than I. As miserable a picture as it may be, the inquiry is mine and mine alone, and that has ramifications far beyond being a technical wonder. Correll stayed a few months, and not long after he left, he died. I heard later that the partner he worked with on the experiments at M.I.T. had even screwed him out of his recognition.

What painting opened up for me is the opposite journey from therapy, especially the type of treatment in which the psychoanalyst invariably wanted to lead me back into the past, often to my first years of life, since that early period is considered to be the time my neurosis was formed as a result of problems I was unable to surmount. Because of those difficulties, I was led to believe, I suffered bitter and painful regret and developed guilt feelings, which are usually transferred to the family. If the problem wasn't the family? No problem, the psychoanalyst was willing to help me find another scapegoat. Instead of combating this situation, the psychoanalyst was always magnifying its importance, which seems a pessimistic doctrine, full of a subtle type of imperialism. I wonder how many obsessions have really been cured by psychoanalysis. I wonder if its record is as good as the intense propaganda campaign for it would have us believe.

The other ring I wear is a silver band I made in Occupational Therapy. For a while there I was ring king. I knocked them out as fast as I could. I even wore the bundle of ring sizes on my belt. I'd jangle them at the aides when they jangled their keys. I'd make anybody a ring whose finger passed near me. The ring remains a talisman for me.

84

That's how I met Barbara. On my way out of the hospital, as a day patient, I still made rings. She wanted one. We became friends. Because I was a day patient living in town, I hated to return. Because I was "out," I could help her by inviting her into town, to be outside for a few hours. Outside contact with my friends had meant a lot to me. However, loving my newfound freedom and wanting to minimize my past associations, I let more and more time elapse between my visits, or calls, to her.

One afternoon, full of anticipation, eager to invite her into town, I called from a pay phone. An aide answered. He put me on hold. Barbara's voice didn't come on, the nurse's did. She said Barbara was dead. She had died in packs two days before. She'd burst a blood vessel in her head and died.

"Just died?" I said.

"Yes, of apoplexy," the nurse said.

Tonight, I found this description of apoplexy in the medical section of Horace Kephart:

> The face is flushed, the lips are blue, the eyelids half open, eyes insensitive to touch, respirations, snoring, pulse full and slow, skin unusually cool, generally one side of the body is paralyzed. The case may or may not be fatal.

Packs are a restraining technique used for your own protection.

❧

Evening.   End of a long day. Waiting for the rice to cook. Nice evening. Clear evening. Silent clouds above me have turned gray, ones on the horizon are red orange. Some corners and edges are still white. The pond in front of me has turned dark. The wind has died.

I'm camped at what is forevermore known as "Denny's Rock," one huge boulder, big as a small house. A Titan's building block standing alone by the edge of this pond.

I'm bivouacking against it under the canoe. I leaned the paddles against the rock, ten feet apart, leaned *Monkey* on them and tied it down. Then I ran the tarp over the canoe to create a space protected from rain. It won't rain. I hope.

This is such a handsome stick-up-in-the-middle-of-nowhere, look-at-me sort of boulder, in the middle of an alpine meadow, I decided to camp here. I'm at the fourth Palmer pond. All afternoon I've been in the soft, undulating world of high alpine meadow. The mountains stepped back, making the meadow seem as vast as the Mongolian Steppes because I've left the intense, narrow world of the lower Palmer valley. The wind creates an ocean feeling blowing through the grass. A flight of sparrows appeared to escort me across the meadow to the pond. They darted, swooped, and circled around me in the steady breeze. I was their meal ticket. They were feeding on the small cloud of mosquitoes and blackflies following in my wake.

The portage was two miles up from the lower pond. The first mile was straight uphill. On a steep pitch, going over wet ground, I slipped. I put my foot on wet moss covering a rock. The tumpline scraped across my face, knocked off my glasses, and caught me in the neck. The eighty-pound wannigan pulled me backward head over heels. The box slipped to one side. I'm lucky I didn't land on top of it. That was bad.

I named the rock for Denny because he would enjoy bivouacking. I think of him a lot. He made a beautiful canoe. When he builds one, first he thinks about it. He found out everything he could concerning my needs, about Labrador's conditions. Each canoe he makes is tailor-made for the person and the use he wants it for. I needed a fast, one-man canoe strong enough to withstand a lot of punishment.

He started with a plywood form for the hull. Then he built the hull around it. He used one-quarter-inch aircraft-grade Sitka spruce for the bottom and clear-grain Western red cedar for the sides. After he sanded smooth the outside hull, he saturated it with a special boat-building epoxy and applied a covering of transparent fiberglass cloth to strengthen *Monkey* against impact and abrasion. When the fiberglass dried, he put on a coat of marine varnish. He repeated the process on the inside of the hull. The gunwales are made from Honduras mahogany, and the bow and stern short-thwarts from ash. He put in one woven cane seat. *Monkey* is incredibly strong, light (fifty-five pounds), and maneuverable. However, the description doesn't capture *Monkey*'s essence, the something no aluminum, plastic, or machine-made canoe has: the beauty a skilled hand transmits to what it creates.

The rhythm of dark cedar strips laid in between the light ones is a joy for me to look at. The ovoid shape is very feminine, very sexy. Denny's attitude toward beauty is not decorative. He doesn't tack it on but draws it from function. He is as much a part of the canoe as I am using it. *Monkey* is a carrier of cargo, a carrier of dreams, a catalyst between the land and the water, a catalyst between the land of day to day and the land of aspiration.

In the Peabody Museum in Cambridge, Massachusetts, and the Museum of Natural History in New York, I love to visit the Inuit and Indian tools, weapons, utensils, and their carvings and masks. Even through glass cases they exude more life than a lot of the art I see. As artistic as they are well suited to their function, they reveal something about their maker's daily life beyond survival: a life limited to essentials includes art.

Fixing dinner, gathering dead twigs and beginning to break them up to make a fire, I was duped into thinking I saw fish. The pond was glass-smooth, except for raindrop circles appearing on the surface. Fish were rising to kiss the top of the water, to suck an insect down. I saw a particularly energetic rise, dropped everything, and ran to the pond's edge. The circles turned out to be gas bubbles, not trout. I was mad at first. Then I laughed. I've been drawing some more fish.

In the mud along the shore were the fresh tracks, feathers, and droppings of geese. It amazes me how everything alive, except the bugs and the caribou, fades out of sight when it hears me coming. I'm quiet traveling alone, much quieter than a group would be. I've seen bear, wolf, and fox tracks, but no animals. I'm sure they are watching me.

The caribou are different. I've come face to face with numbers of them. One almost swam into camp tonight. He was crossing the pond right at me. Because of that large nose leading him he didn't see me. He was almost out of the water before realizing I was there. Instead of altering course, he completely reversed direction and paddled back to the other side.

If I were a suburban, card-carrying, emotional environmentalist, I'd be taking some damning notes on these tundra tanks. It's a scandal the way their paths scar the landscape. Why, they shouldn't be allowed to stay here. Their tracks are destroying a sensitive ecosystem. Just look at the myriad worn paths crisscrossing that slope! The crime is overuse of trails! They should be prevented from doing this, perhaps deported, sent to Florida for half the year. The purity of the tundra is at stake!!

The sun has set. I'm writing by the fire, under the shadow of the boulder. The sky looks like it will remain clear. The evening has a quiet, somber quality. I'm held in twilight, a little darker than it has been, but still not nighttime. The fire pops and cracks. I feed it from a big pile of dry alder twigs and roots beside me. Feeding a fire is a conversation. It's an intimate thing. I've learned a lot about people through their attitude towards fires. Some people throw them together, others are very meticulous arranging the logs. To some people it's a ritual. I don't know why three times, but my habit in lighting a fire is to light it in three different places.

Here I have to use as little paper as possible. I gather dry grass and a selection of various-sized twigs. Lighting the paper under the grass, adding the smallest twigs to that, then adjusting larger ones in the flame until it's caught is how I start.

Today: on the portage between the third and fourth ponds I was higher than a rainbow. First a cloud-shower passed over me. It sank down into the valley, trailing a rainbow. It was as if I walked up under the rainbow's arch to stand a little higher on the mountain. The lower pond and the river were behind it. The rainbow was soft in its colors, pinkish. The light rain made a humming sound as it passed me. It sounded like an old woman humming to herself.

Portaging across the meadow, my eyes focused in front of me, the first Arctic poppy surfaced at my feet. There it was, a two-inch-tall drop of pale gold as fragile and compelling to me as the rose so loved by Saint-Exupéry's Little Prince. I put down my load just to be with it for a minute.

July 21.   No need for an alarm clock, not with a friendly mosquito buzzing in my ear. Up early, breakfast of pancakes and the last of the bacon. Now I'll start to hunt. Three cups of coffee.

Eleven days. One-third the trip. This valley is the most unusual I've ever traveled through. Its steepness, the water-falls, the wind, the rocks, the rockslides have an unsettling, raw power. I feel this rawness more for having entered the softness of the meadow, a contrast to the past eleven days.

Saw my first wolf. Dark colored, lean, with white markings. I felt it was a female. She was twenty yards away. I had a minute watching her lope along before she saw me or smelled the fire. She froze, turned toward me, beetled her ears back and forth in my direction. She was trying to sense danger. When she didn't, she lowered her head and nonchalantly continued on her rounds.

I had been making a watercolor of Denny's Rock when I saw her. What struck me most was the naturalness of her movement. She flowed over the uneven ground, the tufts of grass, the depressions. She was totally at ease, a moving part of the landscape. It made me realize how much I strain to capture the landscape in watercolor. Loosen up. Don't rush. I can open the window but can't invite the breeze in. The question here isn't different from the one in the studio. It is how to proceed. One is no less physical, no less metaphysical than the other.

But the trip has a certain specificity that doesn't exist in

Journal entry. Denny's Rock

Journal entry from lower Korok River

*The two following pages from my journal show how I
often wrote and painted on the same paper.*

the studio. This journey has a map and a definite time limit
— I won't be here in November. And it has a clear goal, to
reach the end of the river. Traveling days are more directed
than my walks. At the end of the day I'll amble off, headed
nowhere in particular. If I get an idea where I want to head,
I usually end up some other place. Yet I always come back. I
will have a lot of satisfaction in reaching the mouth of the
Korok.

Studio time is no less directed, no less full of ambling. The
time frame in the studio is more flexible, like my whole life.
The goal is not specific. It's more an attitude, a way of working, than any specific moment to be achieved. There's no one
painting I can point to and say, "There, that's it." However,
one thing the trip and the studio share is a nuts-and-bolts
attitude. Not the ideas, theories, formulas some people make
them out to be made up of. Painting has to do with expressing a strong temperament. For me it can't be detached
problem-solving or illustrating an elaborate spider web of
theory. The question lurking for me when I attained the ability to create a good-looking object, or negotiate a long canoe
trip, was what to do with that ability. That I can't find out
without proceeding.

Rolling up is now automatic. I don't roll the tent and my
gear together, but separately. The tent fits in its own bag,
which slides into my pack beside my bedroll. My sister, Eve,
made me a denim cloth divided into five pockets. The
different-sized pockets keep my clothes organized and easy to
find. The cloth is cut the same size as the sleeping bag. When
I unroll at night, the rerolled cloth becomes a pillow. In the
morning I unroll the cloth on top of the sleeping bag and
place the three-quarter-length sleeping pad on top of that. I

kneel on it as I roll to make it as tight as possible. To tie it I use two twelve-inch stretchable cords with hooks on their ends.

&

Later. Today has a beautiful texture: quiet, soft, gray. It's as pleasing as running my hand over a cashmere sweater. The wind is holding southwest.

The day started with loose clouds. After my first portage they tightened up. Then they smoothed out to a consistent gray sky. I was traveling the last few miles to the head of the valley, to a place called the Porch.

Getting there was a bitch. Several short portages, then a long carry. I hate short portages. I unload the canoe. I load the canoe. I paddle a hundred yards and do it all again. The river curves left. I portage the inside of the curve. The carry to the Porch was a mile, which means seven for me: take the wannigan over, walk back; take the baby over, walk back; take the pack over, walk back; take the canoe over, and I'm finished.

I carried my first load high up the mountain and came down to the Porch. Picked a campsite up against a five-foot-high rock wall. Beside me was a black pool. I can't see the bottom of it. It must be deep. Lots of brown mosquitoes hover over the black water. By the time I brought *Monkey* to camp, the rain was heavy. Luckily, I'd set the tent up before going back for the canoe.

Several rivers meet here. Each one converges from a different direction. I look down at the last two ponds and across at the peaks I was underneath last week. The Porch is a chasm, an inversion of the peaks. I get a slippery stomach gazing over the edge into the void that makes the gorge. It's a long, thin slit in the earth, the womb of the Palmer River, its head-waters. The water below me is turquoise green. The dominant rock colors are sandy gold and black. Turquoise, gold, and black. The white strips of waterfalls and the more obliquely angled rivers converging here make this a powerful place. It's in the air.

All day I was aware of another inversion. After the sky became gray there was more light on the ground than in the sky. The light-colored mosses and lichen, the patches of light stone, and the pure shots of wildflower color: the blue, yellow, purple, pastel red created the strange sensation of the earth emitting light. As I walked through them I could feel each different color zone as though it were heat, or a texture.

The last eleven days have moved me deeply. Being alone has not been lonely or a hardship. In fact, it's opened my eyes. Simone Weil said something I've never forgotten. She defined love as "the giving of attention to an object." Isn't one slightly less attentive traveling with other people? Wouldn't it be fair to say that a great way to enjoy my friends is in the wilderness, but that the best way to enjoy the wilderness is to give it my complete attention? What have I been on this trip but silent? Silent is not being alone, nor is it necessarily solitude. These three words — *silence*, *solitude*, and *alone* — have occupied me off and on a lot. Alone I am all the time. Silence I slip in and out of. Solitude I have had moments of. The first few days I thought I was alone and silent, but I began to realize I was chattering incessantly in my head — going over all my old tapes: what I should have done, what I will do, won't do, would do, my art, my parents, my lover, my this, my that, my, my, my . . .

I saw what a small field of vision I have. How rich I am in

all the things that the technocratic state has to offer: competition, envy, the desire for "more," jealousy, hypocrisy. It seems so silly here, surrounded by this. What can I do to make it stop? At home there are a lot of people and things to keep me from ever listening to myself. Here the distractions are subtler. If I weren't alert I would be moving continually from one chore to the next, not doing the job so much as creating a chore to distract myself. I decided to see what would happen if I began to listen instead of overriding my moods. I am trying to allow myself to flow along with the bad moods as well as the good ones. I still do a lot of chores, but they're different now from the chores of distraction. I feel in them a certain kind of freedom. Not freedom from something — that would be trading one master for another — but by listening, being silent and attentive, the freedom comes because I'm closer to what I'm doing.

Other than wondering what I'll be eating the last week, and my blisters, I feel fine. Hope the rock wall keeps me secure from the wind tonight. The flamingo is out front, a weather vane spinning in the wind on its one leg.

There's always the question of danger on a trip like this and what to do about it. Bringing a radio is one available precaution. Bernie and I carried an extra eight pounds of shortwave equipment. Once, at the end of the trip, we used it. Just to see if it worked. We couldn't get it to broadcast, but we could receive. What we heard, sitting at the mouth of Chauntry Inlet above the Artic Circle, was a C.B. radio conversation between two drivers stuck in the traffic on the New Jersey Turnpike on a hot August afternoon.

If I fall into trouble and if the radio works, my chances of rescue are improved. I would never carry the extra weight of a heavy radio again. A compromise is an Emergency Locator Transmitter. It weighs one and a half pounds and takes up the same space as a beer can. It broadcasts for seventy-two hours. It can resist up to seventeen hours submerged in salt water. Some models have a broadcast mike. My doubt about radios stems from whether or not they create a false sense of security. Perhaps the knowledge that I have only myself to rely on is a better safety precaution than a radio. I noticed the radio's battery is leaking. I hesitate to test it, but I'd better be able to get a refund if it doesn't work.

I'm in danger all the time, but it's hard to judge how that affects me. As opposed to the first few days when anything could make me anxious, I feel comfortable tonight, confident.

The evening I opened David Bosworth's first envelope, I had camped early on a small beach with a protective stand of willows behind me. I had my Fort Chimo hat on, an orange knitted wool cap with a tassel and a pom-pom. Many Inuit men wear them.

Fixing dinner, I heard a rustle off to my left in the willows. Didn't pay any attention. Then I heard it again. I turned to look. I heard the same rustle behind me, as if someone, or something, watching me shifted its position. I turned again. I was scared. I kept hearing the noise, but could see nothing. Before becoming a dervish, I realized the sound was the pom-pom rolling along the cap's rim. It seems funny now, but at the time it showed me the extent to which I was nervous.

It took a while, but I figured out today is Friday. Friday night. A night to be out on the town. Instead of to town, I went to stretch my stiff muscles. In the drizzling half-light, I walked high to have an overview of the Porch. There was mist around the mountains, rain in the chasm. The gray and black rocks along its sides glistened in the rain. I felt lonely.

I stood at the junction of a huge dogleg. Behind me and off to my right stretched the Palmer Valley. To my left I could see up to the next pond. Beyond that is the Korok. The Korok. Just a five-mile walk away.

To return to danger. All I have to do is make a mistake to suffer severe consequences. That I choose the risk makes all the difference to me. It lightens the thought. Here I'm the one to watch out for. In the city it's different.

For Nick Shields, straightening out his lacrosse equipment in the back of his car proved fatal. After our trip on the Eastmain, he took a year off from Hobart College. He was going to travel, work his way across the country. We said good-bye when he dropped me off in Boston at the end of the summer. Once during the winter he passed through Cambridge, but we didn't meet.

By April he was in San Francisco. He'd been there two weeks. The day he died, he was helping a friend pick up a rug. His friend had gone into the house to get the rug while Nick made room for it in the back of the car. While Nick was leaning into the back of the Vega, straightening things out, a black man named Skullcap walked up behind him. Nick never heard him. He was shot three times in the back. He died instantly, the fourteenth victim of what became known as the "Zebra killings."

The others from the canoe trip gathered with his family two days after Easter at the church in his hometown of Greenville, Delaware. The church was still full of Easter lilies. The first spring flowers were up: red poppies on thin green stems, yellow and white daffodils. We were stunned. I was stunned. Back at his family's house after the funeral, looking for a bathroom, I walked into his room. I saw all his stuff there. That was hard to take. Turning to leave I noticed his different heights marked with a pencil line and a date on the door's edge.

I couldn't make sense out of a death like that. It's suddenness brought home to me that I should do the things I want to do now. Not tomorrow. All the world's potential wouldn't equal what I did today.

His death changed his parents. They gave up their comfortable life working for the E. I. Dupont Company to investigate the legal side of handguns. They wanted to see what could be done about limiting criminal access to handguns. They have helped create a lobby, Handgun Control, Inc., in Washington, D.C., to try to stem the torrent of handguns circulating in the country. It seemed odd to me that they would have to work so hard to accomplish something that makes perfect sense. A handgun's primary, almost sole, purpose is to shoot people. Nick's parents are asking that handguns be considered a privilege, not a right. We are the only country in the world that doesn't think monitoring handguns (not rifles or shotguns) is a reasonable request to make of responsible people who wish to own them. It seemed odd that handgun control would meet with so much political resistance, until I realized what lobbies they were up against. The National Rifle Association and the handgun manufacturers are adamantly opposed to any regulation of their business. Why would a rifle association be so against handgun control? Could it be because the N.R.A. is controlled by gun manufacturers, who would lose a lot of business? The N.R.A. has a huge popular following. It seems to me it misleads its membership by making handgun control an emotional issue and not addressing the problem. The N.R.A. feels the American citizenry is being disarmed. It isn't. Legislation isn't disarming. It has nothing to do with shotguns or rifles or sportsmen or even the ownership of a handgun. Ask a hunter how many times he's gone out to shoot deer or geese with a handgun. Handguns shoot people. Tonight I feel Nick's presence strongly.

July 22.   Beautiful. I'm having a dried apricot, looking at my first view of the Korok.

The Korok. There she is. I can just see a swatch of her way off in the west. A piece of blue tacked to the bottom of the sky, fitted between the distant light blue V's of the mountains.

I woke up in gray dawn and ate breakfast before the sun rose. I watched the wind move its chessmen into place: long windrows of gray clouds. What would be its next move? The rain had stopped. The wind changed and became mild, from the north. It's been easy walking the canoe. I followed a group of caribou cows and calves. The little ones' feet move much faster than their mothers'. They all kept their distance. I went high and stayed high. It's the easiest, driest walking. I crossed numerous streams. Saw the remnants of an ancient tent ring. I could see where prehistoric men had burned their fire. Scraping the ground around it, I uncovered lots of bone chips. I thought about doing more extensive digging, but the sky growled. I felt it was the spirit of the Torngat.

Inverted on my head, the canoe is easy to carry. I have a tump and two paddles to support the weight directly down my spine. The tump is on my head. The top part of the paddle blades rests on my shoulders. By sliding more or less of the paddle blade onto my shoulder, to lengthen or shorten the tump, the canoe's weight can be shifted from my head to my shoulders. By alternating the weight this way, I can carry the canoe over long distances without resting. The paddle shafts tie in front of me to the gunwale, or thwart. Holding the shaft, I control the up/down angle of the bow. On a larger canoe than *Monkey* I'd use the ax as a handle to control the position of the bow by hooking it on the forward thwart and using it as a lever. The hardest carrying is down steep hills or when it's windy. There is little shelter from the wind here. I've learned to give ground and to be prepared to spin around a lot.

A quiet morning. I sit on this east ridge with the sun just now touching my side of the valley. For several hours the west side has had sun. A quiet business, this walking with myself. The canoe creaks, makes rhythmic wood sounds. I like to alternate my hands from the wood of the paddles to the leather of the tumpline. It feels good. I sing sometimes. I practice talking from the back of my throat instead of out the front of my mouth. The painful thing is a mosquito or black-fly landing on my face or hands. Because my hands hold the canoe, it's awkward to slap the bugs. They usually get a good bite. I hate them.

Carrying the canoe makes me think of early memories in cars. As a kid I loved being inside such large machines. The sound the blinker made. At night the click of the headlights' high/low beam. The look of telephone wires looping along as I passed by. Keeping my hand out the window, letting the wind support it. How grown up I felt when I was finally able to rest my elbow comfortably out the passenger's window.

A small truck would be helpful today.

The valley keeps opening up. The mountains seem to be walking away from me. I'm halfway across the five-mile portage with *Monkey*. I've entered the generous sweep of the Korok Valley. It is more open, gentler than the Palmer and less dramatic. The sound of the waterfalls is more distant. In the Palmer, rushing, tumbling water sound was all around me from the first day. Here, silence is flowing in. The walking has been good. I have the small blue rucksack with me. It carries rain gear, lunch, and the gun.

Should I do two loads today? Get it over? Or enjoy being at the head of the Palmer Valley another night? Maybe do another watercolor?

Later. Here I am at the river! Stowed the canoe in the gulch to the left of a stream feeding into the Korok. Ate lunch by the river: some dried apples, cheese, raisins. Found the first signs of modern civilization! An old ketchup bottle and a rusty tin can. Just two items, but they jumped right out at me. I'm ready to amble back to the Porch.

I got excited coming over the last mile. I could see the river, see her bending, meandering, meditating her way through her broad valley. That is how I know rivers.

I reached the Korok and took my three sips of water: one for safe journey, one for good fishing, one for good weather. If I'd had a penny I'd have thrown it in the water.

Returning to camp I followed the stream that flows into the Korok from the Palmer Valley. A sand-bottomed stream with lush green grass by its banks. Not much more than several yards wide. A ptarmigan flew out of the willows. I set up the gun. Then there were two birds. They flew into a rock field. They stayed just out of range. They crawled away or burst into flight at my feet. With a .22 I'd never hit them in the air. They are beautiful birds. They are the bird of the tundra. I've seen robins here but they seem out of place. The ptarmigan in its glider flight, white wings held still and stiff on either side of its brown body, is part of the landscape. A combination of snow and rocks. The birds skim close to the earth. They are of the ground, not like Canada geese, who seem like heaven's best dreamers strung out in their chevron flight. I chased the two birds. Then I gave up. I was tired, happy to head back to camp. I promised myself not to hunt until the bacon was gone. Now that it is, I'll keep an eye out, but I'm not that hungry yet.

I thought about hunger on the walk back. Seeing the discarded ketchup bottle by the river made me think of the one Denny found on our trip on the Eastmain. On my first trip on the Eastmain we lost half the food. That changed us, changed the trip.

We had come to the head of Ross Gorge. A huge gorge on the upper part of the Eastmain. We realized the portage around it was ten miles behind us. We'd read the map wrong. Tired and hungry, drifting close to shore, debating among ourselves what to do, we realized there were six geese between us and the bank. We killed four. We took it as an omen to stay there and camp. Chris White and Nick went to scout the possibility of cutting our own portage. They returned to goose livers, hearts, and gizzards being sautéed in the pan with a little oil, pepper, and salt. They said we'd be able to cut a portage.

The gorge was a dogleg. The following day we cut our way across the hypotenuse. We came out where we thought the gorge ended. We loaded the canoes in a large eddy. Bill Emmons and I followed Nick and Chris around the corner.

Denny and Steve were behind us. As we came around the corner, I saw the red canoe as though I were looking down a long, sloping tunnel. They were tipping over. We were being carried into a set of huge standing waves. With two opposite, split-second actions, Bill pulled for shore and I steered for the smoother water in the middle. We went broadside. Bill stopped paddling to reach for his flotation jacket. I could have hit him. At least you have to try. The first wave hit us. Then the second. We submerged. We still sat in our seats even though the canoe was two feet underwater. Then the current slowly turned the canoe over and threw us out.

It took us an hour to gather what we could and to get to the foot of the gorge and assess the damage. We were lucky to be alive. My canoe was broken badly and half the food sat at our feet, a soggy mound. That night we ate half-a-dozen meals of melted spaghetti. The remaining spaghetti we baked into hardtack biscuits. The next day began two weeks in which we were hungry all the time. We ate half rations. Our stomachs gnawed at us. Each of us gnawed at the others.

Food became an obsession. I dreamed about it. I discussed it in minute detail. We all talked about what we'd eat first when we got out. We talked about all the fresh vegetables, corn, peas, beans, lettuce, carrots, but especially the corn. We talked about all the attributes of the fruit we liked and debated the benefits of different ice creams. I dreamed about the restaurants I'd go to and how I'd relish being waited on. I discussed all this lovingly, even though it hurt. My paddle became a knife, the water a tub of butter. I could spend an hour eating one saltine-sized piece of hardtack, or half an hour lingering over the choices of what spices to add to my meager bowl of goose broth.

We stopped remarking on the beauty of a small stream

entering the Eastmain to analyze what the odds were of catching trout. A goose in flight wasn't poetry. It was a meal, if we could shoot it. Everyone tried to be polite, but small things got in the way. We all thought of ways to defuse our hunger, and ourselves. We were not always successful.

I discovered the prune pit. I'd see just how many hours I could keep one in my mouth, under my tongue, or against the roof of my mouth, all the time anticipating the moment it would break open and the small seed inside would render up to me a delicious moment of pure prune taste.

The saddest incident involved the geese. We had the four geese in our game bag when we tipped over. Because of everything else needing attention, no one bothered to air them out. Several hungry days later a foul, ripe smell emanated from the bag.

We were wind-bound on a beach. Huddled against the bank, crouched out of the wind and rain, we were waiting, just waiting for the wind to die. No one saying much, everyone absorbed in his own thoughts. We were listening to our hungry stomachs. Lunch had been slim: a bit of spaghetti hardtack and a bowl of goose broth.

Denny carried the game bag and was in charge of it. For something to do, he emptied the bag and decided two of the four geese were rancid. He asked if we agreed. Smelling them, we agreed. Did anyone want to pluck them to get what good meat there might be so that we all could get one swallow? No. We were hungry and lethargic, not desperate. Okay, said Denny, I'm bushing the two birds. He walked to the end of the beach and threw them away.

Ten minutes later, Bill walked down the beach, cut two drumsticks off, brought them back to the fire. He started getting ready to cook them. He meant them for himself. We objected. No one eats unless we all eat. "Fuck you" was his response. Chris joined him, cut some meat for himself. Rancid or not, selfish or not, they were going to eat. Only heavy silence from the rest of us followed. The rain and the sizzle of meat in the pan were the only answer to our smoldering silence. We'd been a group until then. After that we were individuals. Hungry ones.

We all showed how hunger breaks down social bonds. A few days later we had to bypass a bad stretch of rapids by going through a series of lakes and down a small river called the Clearwater. On one of the lakes we saw the abandoned A-frame of a camp. We made a beeline to the camp and ransacked it. No food.

Then Denny yelled he'd found their dump. He was up to his hips digging when we reached the side of the garbage pit. There was room for only one person in it. We lined the edge and cheered while Denny handed up what he found. He unearthed an old ketchup bottle with a little left in it. He found a jar of pickles, a syrup can, a moldy bacon. Then he found the prize — a can half full of strawberry jam. We left with an odd assortment of food. Not enough to make a difference to us, but enough to raise our spirits. That strawberry jam caused some heated arguments.

A week later we heard the sound of a motor off the river. An hour later, on a small lake, we met three miners. It was the end of their season. They had plenty of food to share. We ate until we got sick. We threw up and ate again. We were happy to be sick. The food crisis was past, but so was the most real part of the trip. My clearest, sharpest memories remain the days when we were hungry.

～

I'm glad to be at the head of the Palmer one more night. I'm doing one more watercolor of the Palmer Valley. My feet are killing me.

It's hot, calm, and crowded. My dearest northern companions, the mosquitoes and blackflies, have arrived by the thousands. They persist in following me around. Even though I swear at them and kill them a dozen at a time they still come to me. I smell terrible, but they don't care. I changed my Fort Chimo hat for my best bug hat. It's a toque from the island of Madeira. It has earflaps that keep the fucking little bastards out of my ears.

If I could think of a use for mosquitoes, I'd be a rich man. Dante left out one of hell's worst torments by not including a circle in the inferno filled with insects. They are all my evil thoughts returning to attack me. They're terrible.

I've retreated to the tent. Two loads tomorrow and I'm across. I can carry the baby and the pack together. I painted a full-sheet watercolor of the Palmer Valley with a rainbow. Some of the ruggedness of the landscape entered the work. Here I don't have to carry water with me when I paint. I just reach out in any direction. There's bound to be a pool or trickle of water near me. There was a trickle beside me today. Its sound was as clear and distinct as the huge waterfall across the valley. The small, closer sound piggybacked on top of the larger sound.

I watched eight caribou move in single file from the floor of the valley up the other side of the Porch. They appeared so small to me from where I was that at first I thought they were wolves. They never slowed down, whether moving over grass, rocks, on the flat, or going up ledges. They're awkward-looking creatures until they move. Except for the polar bear and the barren-ground grizzly, they're the largest tundra dwellers. They rely on their speed to protect them from their two main enemies: the wolf and man. Even a newborn calf can outdistance a wolf soon after birth. If it can't it dies.

The caribou migrate here in the spring. They come to be in the higher, more open, and more protected land. Here they have their calves and pass the summer in small groups, or on their own. In the autumn they return south, drifting out of the mountains in groups of twos and threes. These bands join larger and larger groups until they become one huge herd. They are headed to the fir forests, their winter feeding grounds. I'm told it's one of nature's most beautiful, majestic sights to see them in migration. The closest I've come was with Bernie on the Back River. We passed the herd's fording spot. We knew it from the amount of hair washed up along the river bank. There were windrows of hair three inches thick on the beach.

A week later Bernie and I saw a sight that made us wonder if the Northwest Territory's herd could continue to thrive. In one of the outbuildings at the abandoned nursing station at Chauntrey Inlet, we found the carcasses of twenty-four caribou. The roof of the building was missing. The only remnant of better days in the building was the huge Toledo scales. The animals covered the whole floor. Only their haunches and front thighs had been taken. Each of their tongues had been cut out, too. The rest had been left to rot. They made a

View from the Porch,
looking back toward Nachvak Fiord

strange, unsettling sight lying there by the scales without their legs. I hope for its sake the Labrador herd is treated with more respect by its hunters.

July 23.   Dreamed of Mandy. Rather, I dreamed of Rome. I couldn't feel farther away from her. She's working in Rome for the summer. My dream was of luxury: glass chandeliers, restaurants crowded with people. Buildings, lemon sherbet served inside scooped-out lemons. Heat. It was terribly hot. I was standing by a fountain with lions' heads spouting water. The sun was setting. The sky above the buildings was alive with swallows or bats. I felt frustrated not knowing any Italian. Yet people came up to me out of the crowd to give me food (pizza; do they have pizza in Italy?) and something cool to drink, even money. But they couldn't tell me where to find Mandy. Then I woke up.

Today. Take the wannigan over first. Check the length of the tump to be sure the headband rests in between my thumb and index finger when my elbow rests on top of the wannigan. Then, by balancing the box on my thigh, tump around the back of my head, I cross arms, right hand grabbing left side of tump, left hand grabbing right. With a swinging motion I turn and shift the wannigan onto my back.

Then begin. Five miles. Don't think about it all at once. It's too much. Think about the first mile. One foot in front of the other. Don't worry about the blisters. Try to forget the pain. A hundred thoughts take over. Have I left everything all right at camp? Have I got what I need for the portage? What's the weather going to do?

Aching from yesterday, I move slowly. Not warmed up yet.

The first mile is straight uphill over rocks. Don't go too far before resting. Follow the caribou path. They usually take the easiest, driest way. Pick out a landmark to aim for. Weight of the box getting to me. Lean farther forward. Occasionally look up to see I'm still on track. Sweat trickles down my side. It feels cold compared to the sweat under my arms. My T-shirt is bunched up under my right shoulder. It hurts. Try to adjust it without putting down the wannigan. Shift weight, stagger, slip. Almost drop the wannigan.

Walking, lead with the hips. Try to, anyway. Place whole foot on the ground. Feel the spread of the toes. Head for the high ground. Avoid the willow clumps, the wet muck. Look for the rock the right height to rest the box on. Not too long a rest. The cool air stiffens muscles. Sweat cooling off. Back at it. Mile after mile. Thoughts become freewheeling. They operate on their own behind my eyes. My eyes are always focused on the next step. One foot in front of the other, one foot in front of the other . . .

After several miles I'm numb. I travel on automatic pilot. I try not to stop. If I stop, I only have to start again. Even so, I can't resist that rock. Every muscle screams. Rest. Take a few sips of sweet water, wash my face. Kill a few mosquitoes. Begin again. I feel each different texture of the landscape beneath my feet. The large, loose rocks at first, the stream-bed smooth rocks, the moss fields, the bog with its knotted tufts of grass, the flat patches of gravel, the unstable piles of jagged rocks, the clusters of wildflowers, the yards and yards of ground cover, which crunches underfoot. The sucking sound of my feet going in and out of the muskeg.

Rest.

With the weight off my back comes a rising sensation. It's as if I were floating. The landscape takes on a surreal quality.

It appears stiller and more silent than it's ever been. Even in the strong wind, nothing moves. My breathing becomes the loudest sound.

Begin again.

Each mile peels off onionlike layers of thought. Thoughts about places, about people I haven't remembered for years.

I'm feeling the split in me between the country and the sea. I always felt I wanted to live in a place that had both. Ireland seemed an ideal. I had talked my way into college at the University College, Cork. I spent my junior year from Harvard there studying painting and poetry, particularly the poet-painter David Jones. The dean at Harvard said to me when I went in to tell him of my opportunity, "Mr. Perkins, most people try to get to Harvard, not leave it." But I went.

I traveled with Wendy. We were renting a small house in Gyleen for ten dollars a week. We were friends with the owner of the Bridge House restaurant, Enid Hague. During the few weeks we stayed there she was always asking us if we had enough. We helped her in the kitchen. She gave us magnificent leftovers.

One evening, walking after dinner, we climbed the hills behind Gyleen. The hills were bare. They seemed an extension of the sea, as if they were waves that had been turned into hills. They were overgrown with blackberry hedges and fuchsia bushes. The sea to our left, the village soon dropped behind us. We were walking a path parallel to the sea. We saw a tall ruin of a wall. I ran to it. I climbed it. On top, with my arms open, the breeze in my face, I looked out to the sea. At first my eyes were drawn to a tangle of bushes. Then I saw the roof and chimney. Nestled in the small protected palm of a hillside was a cottage facing the sea. I climbed down and told Wendy.

Walking up the path into the farm, we came first to the outbuildings. Then into the diminutive courtyard of what had not long before been a working farm. The yard was defined by the house on one side, an overgrown rose garden on another. A crescent-shaped stone wall faced the sea. One stunted tree, sculpted to the contour of the hill by the savage winter winds, stood in the courtyard. I could throw a rock into the sea from the stone wall. We walked through the two-and-a-half-room house and followed the flagstones laid out between the tangle of rosebushes. The garden was run-down in every respect except its beauty. The roses still breathed a delicious aroma. We lingered that evening in its spell.

Together to pick the blackberries and separately to be alone with the house, the courtyard, and the garden, we returned. We talked about owning it. What we would do to support ourselves. Many things held us back, not only our lack of money and an unwillingness to commit our lives to Ireland, but our unwillingness to commit ourselves to each other. Perhaps we knew the home we had found and the love we shared had their beauty in their present tense, in that moment, not in ownership. Perhaps.

My thoughts keep coming: who I like, why I like them, what I want to do with my life, what fresh vegetables I'll eat when I get home. I'm lonely. That explains why I'm remembering so much. The pain of the weight on my back takes over. The mechanics of walking begin to override every other thought. Reach the end. Reach the end . . . my legs, my lungs, my arms, stomach, head all want one thing: the end.

With the Korok in sight the load seems to lighten. I begin to take shortcuts. I cut across wet places I'd have avoided an hour before. Up, down move my legs. They don't seem to be my legs anymore. I sink up to my knees in a bog. Back out. Stagger. Feet take over: up, down, up, down, up, down, and then finally, there. Collapse.

After a long rest, I walk back the five miles. I take my time, I enjoy the afternoon sun. I look for the patches of wildflowers and go out of my way to walk through them. I take mental notes for the next trip about easier ways of crossing certain obstacles. I see a caribou silhouetted on a ridge. I walk toward him. The wind is blowing toward me. I begin to get close. He appears not to mind. Is he a vision? He's facing me, looking right at me. Wouldn't it be great to ride a caribou? Ten yards separate us. He bolts. His silhouette made him appear to be facing me when actually he was looking the other way. He didn't smell me or hear me.

Back at the head of the Palmer. A choice. I could spend another night, or roll up and take the pack and the baby together.

The second trip is twice as painful. Every time I put down the pack, or stumble, the baby falls off. I can't lift them together. I can't bend down for the baby with the pack on my back without risking a fall. If the baby slides off, I have to find a high rock to rest the pack on, then go back for the baby, bring it to the rock. Next I put the pack on, slide the baby on top of the pack by bending forward and pulling it over my head. I laugh at myself. Sing. Rest. I am a piece of pain. Every other sensation is dull in comparison.

In the middle of a bog I reach a low rock. I throw the pack and baby off and slump down on the rock and cry. Wail. Not even with energy. I don't have any. I gurgle. Moan. Why am I trudging around in the middle of nowhere? In the last two days I've walked twenty-five miles, half of them with a load on my back. Deadly, absolutely deadly. There's no glory in this bullshit, believe me.

Later.   Windstorm outside. Tent shaking badly. Sky gray, clouds blown as though the wind is pulling taffy. Severe wind like the storm the first week. Rain and a dark sky overwhelm the land. For the moment a four-foot gully protects me from the wind's full force. When I crawled in I lay on my back. I felt raw, exhausted. A black fever to match the outside weather washed over me. All I could feel was the blackness outside, the endlessness of wind and rain striking at the land. The only thing keeping my black thoughts in bounds was thinking of the wildflowers — those bright, small shots of color in this giant's landscape. Closed my eyes and saw the poppy, the river beauty, the bluebells of Scotland, the pink pincushions. The flowers give the tundra its light touch.

Not feeling well. Want to sleep. Can't sleep. Think of something else. . . .

The Athenaeum. Some people call to make reservations. They think it's a Greek restaurant. But for most Bostonians the word is full of history, connotations, associations with the past, marble statues, plaster casts, old furniture, old pictures, old vases, old tables. One huge table is solid mahogany brought back from China as ship's ballast.

It is the Boston Athenaeum. Pride of Beacon Hill, monument to centuries of Yankee acquisitiveness. Devoted to the past, to the desire to preserve, to hold on to. Each passing year makes its existence more removed from the world around it. Like the tundra, its existence is in jeopardy.

It is run by a ruffle of reference librarians, a director, his secretary, a bursar, a conscience of conservators, a card of cataloguers, a sweet and sour front desk, and an art department. And then there is the Cecil B. De Mille–sized supporting cast of thousands upon thousands of books. Frank always meets me in his studio after work saying, "How's life in the book morgue?"

It is where I've worked for four years. A place of the past. A place of closure, secure as a Jules Verne hero. I can't imagine anything further removed from me here in this tent.

The two disparate things I am a bridge between are the primal here and now and the civilized, the human, the Athenaeum. There's too much reverence for the white hairs in Boston. The question is how to proceed, not how best to hold on. The desire to hold on and the desire to proceed are mutually destructive.

Anger. I'm standing on the steps by the Shaw Monument near the top of Beacon Hill. It's getting dark. Anger. I feel it. It desires the dark. I need a large umbrella to live on top of in Boston. Not to protect me from above but from the festering under my feet. Where is the anger during the day? Not too far away. Every night, like the tide, it returns. The churches are black with it. People's faces are locked up with it. Anger and fear. We've been afraid too long. It grows, rests in corners, sits behind locked doors — anywhere the gray, smooth stone surrenders, where pockmarked faces offer it a hold. Moisture it feeds on. From winter to summer green, it only turns to its back for one and on its belly for the other season. I'm scared.

One sun-flooded church morning as I was lying in bed, the phone rang and rang and rang. I stayed in bed, but I was awake. Soon, I was putting on the kettle, running a bath. My lover stayed in bed. I stood in the kitchen door watching the sun pour into the living room of 14 Union Park Street. The light was warm, smooth, abundant. Had to eat breakfast there, in that light. The light poured over us as we ate. We sat by the window, across from the Greek Orthodox church, catty-corner to the Catholic cathedral. We listened to the bells ring in the faithful. For our service we had three kinds of jam: marmalade with ginger, red raspberry, and Victoria Plum Preserves. And lots of toast. What I wouldn't give for a piece of toast tonight.

Camus this and Kant that. I think the way I travel. Alone is not a group. A canoe is not a jet. Words and paint didn't create the world, but do I have any other choice?

PART
TWO

~~~~~

Come live within me, said the waterfall.
There is a chamber of black stone
High and dry behind my stunning life.
Stay here a year or two, a year or ten,
Until you've heard it all,
The inside story deafening but true.

JAMES MERRILL, FROM *McKane's Falls*

July 24.   The Korok. Breakfast. What a glorious institution, best meal in the day. A cup of coffee, stewed apples and prunes, pancakes with a delicate syrup of apple juice with a little honey. Honey. All them bees. Crystallized honey doesn't drip on everything. I like the way Charles Marz packs his in tins. I carry five pounds as well as three three-pound wheels of sharp Black Diamond cheddar cheese. Just beginning the second one. By the swollen look of the third wheel, it should be plenty sharp by the time I open it.

After last night the sky is an ocean of deep gray waves, all the way back to both horizons. I can see both horizons: up the Korok Valley to where the river begins and down the valley where I'm headed. In the Palmer Valley I saw only a slice of sky, saw the weather when it arrived.

Even though there's a head wind and rain coming, I can't resist pulling a few miles downstream. I remember the description of Rat and Mole on their picnic, watching Toad pass by in his new scull. That's how I'll probably look in the water for the first few days, all commotion and noise, my enthusiasm far outstripping my control.

Later.   What a pleasure to paddle! To drift in the current, and not walk against it. The river is shallow, meandering through what could be an exotic golf course, all rough and sand traps. The banks are low enough for me to see over while sitting down. I had to be careful to stay in the channel to avoid the sandbars. Not a strong current. Shallowness prevents me from taking deep strokes.

Before starting this morning I opened David's next envelope. It was a poem that went:

> *I was always one for being alone,*
> *Seeking in my own way, eternal purpose;*
> *At the edge of the field waiting for the pure moment;*
> *Standing, silent, on sandy beaches or walking along green*
>   *embankments; . . .* *

I didn't like it. It sounded like an old romantic's poem. It is a bunch of hooey. It did make me realize that in the midst of this man-silent world, where my concerns are right in front of me, where to camp, what to eat, how to portage, David's quotes are a voice from another reality.

Afternoon.   Fish. Brook trout! I caught a fish! Even if it's only six inches long, I caught one.

Being on the river was great. Paddling against a head wind was not. I came to a beautiful narrows, a waist in the river,

---

* Theodore Roethke's "Meditations of an Old Woman," from the "Fourth Meditation."

where the right side was a steep sand esker plunging into the water, a perfect windbreak. What should be standing on the crescent of sand but a bull caribou. He jumped when he saw me. He started to leave, but changed his mind, looked again, and then left. He bolted straight up the esker like a small tank. He stood a minute at the top for a last look and a disapproving snort. I let the current drift me through the narrows. I didn't want to break the silence of its magic.

Around the corner I met a cold head wind. I turned back to pull into the crescent of beach. I'd brew a cup of tea, wait to see if the wind died. Sand is the flesh tone in the landscape.

Shouldn't I stay? There might not be many protected spots ahead. Then I saw a rise next to *Monkey*. Bernie wouldn't have approved, but I set up the spinning rod with a small Dardevle lure. I hooked one right off. He threw the hook on the beach and bounced and flipped into the water. I couldn't call him the first fish. Caught another, a gleaming, light-colored, six-inch trout. I let him go. Something superstitious, but I release the first fish of the summer. Then I kicked myself as I couldn't catch another and got hungrier and hungrier. Without getting mad, I put down the rod and went to make camp.

I watched them rise as I set up the tent, built a fireplace, gathered willow twigs for the fire, and prepared dinner. I measured half a cup of rice out, half a handful of raisins, a few cashews, and put them into the pressure cooker. I cut a wedge of cheese to melt into the rice later. I ate a piece of candied ginger as an appetizer. All the time I could hardly take my eyes off the water.

I was making myself wait until the chores were done. One chore was to check the rice supply. It's half gone. I doubt I'll overeat this trip.

I was luckier fishing the second time and caught two. They made a welcome addition to the rice. They're spooky fish, hard to catch. On the Back River, all we had to do was look at the water to catch fish. Granted, they were the ugliest trout in the world. Their heads were huge in proportion to their bodies. Big ones that looked more like pike than trout. Not like these beautiful, little trout.

As the sun set, the wind died. The evening became quiet. The last light had the same effect as a snowfall; a stillness settling over everything. I could hear the hum of mosquitoes on the other side of the river, the occasional plop of a trout surfacing. No deafening waterfalls here.

I climbed the esker in the tracks of the caribou to watch the sun set. On top I was two hundred feet above the river. Nothing nearby was half as high. What an inversion from the Palmer Valley! The sun set, but the light lingered on different spots as if reluctant to leave them. The river below me became a sheet of iridescent, twisted silver laid on the darker landscape. Off to my right I could see black spots on the silver. They were the rocks of the river's first rapids. The evening's stillness allowed the rapids' deep rumble to drift up to me on the esker. The calmness of the evening settled in my stomach next to the trout.

The silence of rocks is staggering. In a forest, even in a field, I am distracted from noticing them by the movement of the grass, or the trees. Activity and the earth often hide them and their beautiful, endless silence. Driving along highways between where the engineers have blasted through a hill I see bare rock, yet the vertical core-hole scars from the driller and the jagged, exposed rock edges blown apart by dynamite are a scream; not like this.

Passing through the head of the Palmer Valley, I saw more

rock than I expect to see again. It's the closest I'll come to the snow patches on the mountains, too.

July 25.   Dream. Fishing/art. In a boat with Craig and Karl. Craig is a sculptor and Karl is a musician. They're good friends. I was using what I thought was a Dardevle, but later I found out it was a floating minnow. I was catching fish. No one else was. I told Karl to put on a Dardevle. He didn't like the suggestion. He told me so. Feisty Karl.

Then we were on a pier. A long pier. More fishing. This is where I see I'm using a minnow. Craig catches fish. Then, letting my lure drift under the dock into the shade, I get one huge strike. I have too much line in my hand to let go of it and use the reel. Instead, I pull with my hands, like a hand-line. Bob Neuman helps pull. He's the first painting teacher I had who taught me anything. I play the fish a long time. This all takes place in front of a party boat full of people watching. (Thought: as I remember the dream images they evoke associations, the same way an object does when I look at it while I'm awake. In a sense, the object in my dream is as real to me as the tent is. My associations operate the same way toward a dream image as they do toward an object in the physical world.) When I get the fish up on the dock, I see it is a green, ugly piece of kelp. Karl says it's a skunk. I tell him it's a piece of kelp, but it turns out to be a skunk. I cannot believe it. Immediately I'm sorry I went fishing because I caught a skunk instead of a fish.

Later.   Amazing day. I almost ended the trip in the first set of strong rapids. I swamped.

All morning the rapids were more rock than water. Bone-yards; terrible tilting, shallow, rock-dodging, tight-maneuver-ing sons of bitches. They went on for miles. This is how it happened. . . .

After leaving camp at the narrows, I run two miles in fast current and open, shallow water. I turn a corner and surprise at least twenty geese. There is no chance for them to fade silently away. Still molting, they honk and awkwardly flap away, half of them going inland, half downstream. They can't actually fly when they're molting. They escape danger two ways: by staying in the river, or hiding on land. In the river they can stay submerged several minutes, reversing direc-tions and outdistancing me underwater. They can lay their necks along the water and paddle. They are especially hard to see when they do this if there's a wind of any kind making waves. On land they run extremely fast, again holding their necks horizontal to the ground. They squat when they find a place to hide. They effectively become just one more mottled piece of the landscape. Unless I step on one, they won't give themselves away.

The chase is on. I go for the ones on land. I race *Monkey* to shore. I only run the canoe into one rock. I set up the .22, plunge into the willows along the shore. Two ptarmigan fly up. I shoot one. He would be one meal caught up on my dwindling rich supply. I put the bird behind me under the seat.

I paddle on. I can see geese scattering silently up the op-posite bank. One stays in the river acting as a decoy while the others fan out into the tundra. The decoy thinks he is luring me downriver, away from his friends. He stays close enough to me to make me feel I can get closer. Feigning injury until he judges we are far enough away from the others, he awkwardly lifts himself over the surface of the water and makes a wide circle around me, heading upstream. He honks raucously to his friends about what a fool he's made of me.

It is after that that I come to the first diddly-squat rapids. There isn't enough water between rocks for *Monkey* to maneuver. I'm out of the canoe half the time, pulling, pushing, scraping, cursing, saying to myself, Why aren't I portaging? Just ahead it always looks to be better water but never is. I'd get through a hundred yards and paddle ten before the next rock field. I know if I get *Monkey* stuck on a rock the current could swing the canoe, tipping the gunwale underwater and filling it like a glass. I don't want that to happen. Then it does. The canoe fills. I go to shore, wet and angry. I unload, empty the water, reload. Shoot some more. Rather, I push, pull, and curse my way through more rocks. This continues all morning. In several hours I travel only two miles. I can imagine it would be even tougher traveling later in the season. The water would be even lower, the rocks even harder to get around.

Finally, I hear the healthy rumble of a larger rapid. I bridge *Monkey* between two rocks and climb the ridge to scout it. At last a good set. Stay on the inside curve. Put the spray cover on. No problem, a pleasure to be looking over the first shootable rapids of the trip.

Hopping rock to rock back to *Monkey*, I think of the times people have chastised me for not tying everything into the canoe, their rationale being if I tipped over, I wouldn't lose anything. I've never liked that idea. Even without anything in it a canoe is a heavy, unwieldy, and dangerous object. It is more so when full of water. If I'm caught between it and a rock I could easily be crushed. A canoe with tied-on appendages becomes doubly dangerous. It's easier for me to stay with an unloaded canoe and pick up my gear later.

Back at *Monkey* I look behind the seat. No ptarmigan. I must have put the bird on a rock when I emptied the water out and then forgotten him. He is miles behind me now. What makes me mad isn't wasting what I'd shot (a bear or fox would find him) but my forgetfulness. That scares me. There's no one to help me think.

I snap on the spray cover for the first time. What a sexy-looking thing it is. A big red triangle with a thin black dart reaching a third of the way into it. The cover is three-quarter length, stopping in front of my seat. I've never liked the constricted feeling of a full spray cover. There are times in rapids when I like to stand up and kneel in quick succession. If I come to a patch of smooth water it allows me a second to stand and see what comes next. Other times I'm constantly shifting position from on my knees to sitting on the seat.

The first rapid of the trip. I'm shaking. I enter the V I've chosen to begin my descent. I can feel the butterflies in my stomach. Everything happens fast: pull right, paddle, back-paddle, crack, slide over a rock, keep going, cross over, sweep, paddle, then I'm around the corner.

Around the corner?

What corner?

An all-white wave line appears across the river. Huge standing waves. I can't see the other side. I'm too far from shore. Have to go through them. What to do? Back-paddle to slow *Monkey* down. Try smothering the standing wave. The turbulence yanks the paddle out of my bottom hand. Don't paddle. Balance. Weight back. Wave over the bow. Another. Throw my weight farther back. Try to keep the bow up. Another wave lands in the canoe. *Monkey* sluggish. Water up to my ankles. Can I make it to the back-eddy? Barely. I jump out in knee-deep water, pull *Monkey* to shore. Unload every soggy thing. Heft the canoe out. First the bird, now this. Calm down.

Start to shake. Make some tea. Collect willow twigs. Light the fire: match to the wrapper of a tea bag, some dry grass, smallest twigs on top of that, then feed larger ones, a little breath. Then a few deep breaths to calm me. Just because the sun is out doesn't mean I'm safe.

Drinking my tea I look down my front. The bluebell picked for my buttonhole is still intact. I concentrate on letting its small beauty warm me and dispel my trembling.

I keep the small tea fire company until it dies. I concentrate on its movements: the quick flames, the slower crumble of the wood, the even slower pulse of the embers, the embers' slower change from red to white ash as the fire dies out. I'm glad to be here. Glad to be alive.

The afternoon is more shooting, scraping, hopping out, pulling, and cursing through tight, rocky rapids. No more large ones. No more mistakes. It seems that first one was there to give me a warning.

By late afternoon I'm comfortable "walking" the canoe down this type of rapid. If the river bends, I stay on the inside curve where there's less power in the water. I back-paddle into the V's. By kneeling in front of the seat, putting my knees where the bottom begins to curve into the side, I create a solid triangle to shift my weight around. I control the sharpness of my turns by how much I lean into them. I hit hard on a few rocks but *Monkey* holds up. Those first two weeks walking up the Palmer Valley got me used to *Monkey* and myself, got me into shape, but paddling stretches a whole different set of muscles. I ache as though I'd begun the trip yesterday.

The short bird's-eye maple paddle I've had for years developed two three-inch splits in its tip. I put a lot of stress on the blade pushing off the bottom, or using it to absorb the impact of a rock. Splits eventually break the blade. The simplest fix-it is to hammer in two wood staples. I put one at either end of the split. These keep it from lengthening, without adding extra weight to the blade. The back of the ax head is my hammer, the nearest rock the anvil.

I carry three paddles. Each one is a different length. Each one is a piece of hardwood. My favorite is bird's-eye maple. Compared to my six-foot-two height, it's short by conventional canoeing standards. It's only four feet ten inches tall. The blade is ovoid, the handle pear-shaped. When I bought it, the paddle was totally varnished. To avoid blisters, because the shaft constantly twists in my grip, I sanded the varnish off the handle and off an eight-inch strip along the shaft above the blade. After an initial oiling, my hand's natural oil keeps the wood from drying out. Over a long trip the constant, short pry used in the J stroke against the side of the canoe wears down the gunwale as well as a spot on the paddle. I'll be filing and sanding frayed wood before the trip is over.

Paddle technology has created endless variations in design and materials. However, the major advance is one of durability. Today there are indestructible paddles. Tempting as bringing one on this trip was, durability was only one factor. In addition to paddling, I need paddles to carry the canoe. The aluminum-shaft paddles with plastic blades may be indestructible, but I couldn't use them to portage comfortably with. The wide blade would not fit my shoulders or allow me to slide them forward when I need to shorten the tump.

In white water, a wide blade for the bowman can be helpful, especially to "draw" the canoe right or left, but it tends to grab and hinder a sternman's strokes. By pulling against more surface area, wide blades move the canoe through the water faster. They're ideal for racing, but they tire me quickly. Over an eight- or ten-hour day, I prefer to keep the tortoise's pace.

I paddle a J stroke. It combines a forward stroke with a pry. The first part of the stroke pushes the canoe forward. The end of the stroke, the pry, holds the canoe on course while adding one last little kick. People who don't use this stroke seem to work harder than they need to. Of the two common ways people make the J stroke, one is to turn their top wrist out and away from the canoe (this is their left hand if they paddle on the canoe's right side). They bring their top arm back toward themselves to make the pry. Although it seems a more natural movement, it actually slows the canoe down. It creates a back-paddle as the blade's edge moves through the stroke. The other method gives that added push forward. I turn my wrist over the paddle with my left-hand thumb pointing toward the bow. This stroke continues the push of the water's flow as it travels by the side of the canoe.

Shooting a rapid is intense, focused work. It helps me to glance away for a second, to rest my eyes. This afternoon, maneuvering in a rapid, I raised my eyes and saw my first small spruce tree. Like a dwarf it squatted near the bank regarding me. What a surprise, a tree!

Monkey and I camped when we could see the first solid finger line of trees ahead. I'm just opposite what's marked on the map as Mt. Haywood. Tomorrow I'll leave the tundra; I'll end one trip and begin another.

The shape of the fir tree, wider at the bottom and reaching to a point at the top, resembles a flame, a frozen, green flame.

I've found a protected camp, but I wasn't the only one looking to get out of the wind. All the flying denizens of the North, the blackfly, the mosquito, and the horsefly, were there to greet me. I can tell how bad they're going to be by how many steps away from the river I get before they arrive. I took three steps. If there's a wind, they hover on my down-wind side and have to work to reach me. If there's no wind and the afternoon sun is warm, they cluster around me. I took out my Madeira toque again, the one with the earflaps. The flaps keep the blackflies out of my ears. I can't imagine anything worse than a blackfly caught inside my ear, its high-pitched whining becoming magnified a hundredfold. My beard acts as another line of defense to keep them off my face.

I put several staples in the paddle and did other chores I wouldn't have done if I hadn't swamped. I brushed my teeth, aired my sleeping bag, oiled my boots, filed the canoe's middle thwart to allow the wannigan to fit more easily between the forward and mid-thwart. Then I filed the wannigan's four corners so the spray cover fits more smoothly over them.

The last day in Stockbridge, we cut the spray cover from heavy, red pack cloth. I traced the position of the snaps on the cloth as Denny had built them into the side of the canoe. We brought the material downtown to a leather shop where they had a grommet machine to fasten the snaps to the cloth.

Usually spray covers fit flush across the gunwales. My wannigan stands three inches higher and we had to find a way to allow for the extra cloth, yet have the material remain taut. Denny's wife, Beck, found the right material to make a dart with: a woman's one-piece bathing suit. The material stretches in all directions. The dart of black bathing-suit material is sewn into the bottom of the spray cover, allowing it to stretch over the wannigan yet keep its shape. This gives the cover its sex appeal.

After chores I set up the fly rod, ready to enjoy my afternoon off. The steep bank behind me didn't allow for back-casting. Instead of fishing toward the middle of the river, I practiced roll and side-arm casts along the bank. I'd see a rise and try to land my fly in the center of expanding circles. These are spooky fish. I couldn't catch one. An added challenge was the strong current. If the fly is being pushed down-stream on top of me, it's hard to catch up on the slack in the line. If I'm retrieving the fly upstream, the fly, even a wet fly, tends to ride on the surface and looks more like a motorboat than an insect.

I wanted fish for dinner. I switched to the spinning rod. With it I could reach the deep water toward the middle of the river. The lure's extra weight keeps it down where the fish are. Soon I caught two ten-inch trout.

Mt. Hayward is like a huge table. It rises alone out of the valley. Because of this and my distance from it, it has none of the drama of the mountains in the Palmer Valley. It marks the entrance of a river flowing into the Korok Valley from Saglek Fiord. It indicates the beginning of trees. The plane created by this swath of fir trees is a deep forest green, a darker green than the light moss green of the tundra's ground cover. I'm very excited to see trees, but sad to be leaving the pure tundra.

One new sensation I enjoy is gliding over endless amounts of rocks. The water is crystal clear and in *Monkey* I see the rocks passing effortlessly underneath me. For so long each rock meant an unstable step, a possible fall. Now I dodge them in the river or pass over them on a cushion of water. Their dry-land gray, black, and dust colors change to rich browns, deep blacks, and creamy toffee, shimmering as the water surface trembles, the colors flickering as if in candle-light.

I'm out of watercolor paper. The last few days I used up the last pages experimenting with the burnt-paper technique. I stumbled on the fact that fiberglass paper doesn't disintegrate when I set it on fire. I've gained control over it and was just becoming expert at making mountain shapes, when I ran out. A friend gave me a roll of paper I thought was individual sheets. This afternoon I opened it up. It's one continuous roll. I turned *Monkey* over and unrolled a piece the length of the canoe, taped it down, took a deep breath, and painted a scroll of my journey.

For the second day in a row the evening is calm and silent. Tomorrow, if it's like this, I'll make a day of it, take a long rest at lunch while the wind is blowing, then travel into the evening.

I've got to be more careful. I can't go around shooting birds then leaving them behind. It creates bad karma.

※

July 26.   Evening. Tired. Late. With the forest comes a whole new world.

The fiberglass core of some of the paper I carried allowed me to experiment with a new medium: fire. I'd create the shapes I wanted by burning the paper.

July 27.   Morning. Yesterday, huge, mountain-sized fair-weather clouds marched across the sky. The rapids were fun. The river opened up.

Water: it's not only in the river. What's a cloud but water? Thousands of minuscule droplets traveling undecided, halfway between the air and water. How many times have I felt like that, half one thing, half another?

River: water traveling as calm, steady order, then tumbling into loud chaos through rapids and settling down again to order. Yet, a rapid is order. The humping waves, the rocks, the V's, the standing waves stay where they are. They never move. It's the noise and power of the water against the rocks that sounds and looks like disorder. Always the river remains indifferent to me.

I came as far as Naksarulak Brook and camped under a knoll surrounded by trees. TREES. Protection from wind and storm. What a luxury. After camp was in order and lunch packed, I entered the forest.

Technically, it isn't a forest. It's a thin belt of trees along the river extending no deeper than a mile back from the water. Beyond that I'm in the tundra again. However, not having seen trees in a while, it's a forest. It's as mysterious and private and closed in and punctuated with pockets and stripes of sunlight as any forest. The dead needles, the decaying trees, and the moss make walking soft and silent; except on the caribou moss, where my steps make the dry-crunch sound of walking on hard-packed snow.

The trees surround me. They bring the feeling of space in on top of me. Even trees no taller than twelve feet make me feel enclosed in a different way than the Palmer Valley did.

The geometry of vertical shapes and horizontal branches hold me spellbound. All the lines in front of my face, the swoop of a hill farther away, the overlay of one tree trunk against another. All the small, shaded glens, open spaces, and dense tangles hide things differently than the exposed mountains that swallow things whole in their immensity.

Spent the afternoon walking slowly to the first rapids on Naksarulak Brook. I walked on the left side of the brook, staying high on a ridge just inside the upper limit of the trees. I heard several caribou, but didn't see them. I found piles of ptarmigan droppings, but not the birds. I could hear the wings of smaller birds around me, but rarely saw them. I remembered a story by H. G. Wells called "The Country of the Blind." In it, the blind inhabitants of a lost valley think birds are angels. No one has ever seen a bird. They hear them sing and hear their wings, but they never catch them.

How different I feel here. Everything is more private, hidden. To get my bearings I'd just surface onto the tundra above the tree line. I was surrounded by the moss's soft, light greens. Among the darker bands of green trees winding ribbonlike up the mountains toward the gray-black rock faces of the exposed, highest ledges, there'd be little clumps of pines in peculiar places. They appeared as though they'd marched away from their companions in a huff. After seeing where I was, I'd reenter the forest; become enveloped in pine smells, the broken light, my frequent, small changes of direction. I'd move through different textures: a clump of tamarack, across a rock patch, among the alders, across moss clearings, acutely aware of each new sensation as though I were a swimmer feeling changes in water temperature.

At the rapids I ate lunch and headed back. I walked near the brook this time. There were long, still pools, backwaters the brook created as it neared the river. The air above them was full of just-hatched insects. In water not deeper than three inches darted hundreds of tiny trout. They were surfacing and jumping after the insects. They were greedy and crazed by the surfeit of bugs. When they weren't jumping, only their shadows over the muck gave their presence away. I stood watching a long time. I felt like a heron. Inside my head I often feel poised over my thoughts, as the bird is motionless over the water, ready, waiting to spear the smallest thought that may come out.

This was the day I'd promised myself a bath. The water was cold, but the afternoon sun was warm. I fell asleep on the rocks for a mosquito-free hour.

Woke up depressed. Don't know why. I thought going fishing would pull me out of it. I set up the spinning rod. The first cast I lost a lure. Felt worse. I had to walk back to camp for another lure. I slipped off a rock and got my feet wet. The sun was going down. I felt close to losing it, close to confusion, my darkest thoughts. I turned all my attention to fishing. I focused on that lure; moved with it through the water. One side is painted red and white, the other side is silver. In the current it can spin without my reeling in line, if I hold it there. The river was deep, the rocks stuck up almost to the surface. In between them were the deep, protected hiding places. I let the lure hover over these holes. I began to catch fish. My spirits improved. I had several trout with my pancakes.

Curious that I haven't caught a large trout. They've all been half a pound or less. I had expected to catch good-sized fish. I'm sure they're here. The Korok certainly hasn't been overfished.

I haven't enough oil to grease the pan with. My discovery

is that with a hot pan the pancakes won't stick. They cook more quickly and come out a golden brown. Tonight I feature corncakes. That's cornmeal mixed with a touch of whole-wheat flour for body, salt, a hint of baking powder, and water. Cooked, they look like lace doilies.

It's too bad I'm not temperamentally a realist landscape painter. Then the expedition and my studio time would share a consistency they don't appear to have. I'd be the archetypal Romantic artist. But I'm not. I feel close to that northern European sensibility. I admire the Americans and Europeans who painted the landscape as they saw it rather than as European convention dictated it be painted. It's what they discovered on their own, what they didn't do right, that makes their paintings so good.

Tonight I've been watching the river as the light leaves it. At which second, at which angle of light to paint it? What to paint isn't any particular frame of time, but the flow of time from the blue-green when the sun is still on it to the almost black it is now.

What has grown inside me from the first day is the waterfall. A line. A seeming-void-down-the-mountain-face. The always-moving, never-changing flow of a vertical river. A river connecting heaven to earth. Eternally a masculine/feminine force that gathers and feeds itself. A sound as well as a sight. Forever new but always contained in the same form. The linelike quality of it in the distance. The overpowering envelopment of it close up. The water flowing underground, falling into pools, circling, pouring down. The sound-fall accompanying it.

Tomorrow, on to the one big fall actually in the Korok. I'll spend a day or two there, fishing for the king of trout.

July 28.   Korluktok Falls. Didn't use the map. Short day. Several rapids. Two portages around large rapids. Felt good traveling without constant reference to a map. I kept expecting the falls to be around the next corner. Anticipation. This corner? No. This one? No. Then there it was . . . the mist circling up, the noise. I pulled out above it. I walked down to look. It's tall and wide and huge. It's so loud, there is no room left in my head for any other sound.

I came to the edge, close as I dared, and looked at the drop: a smooth, thick curve of water dropping over the edge. It falls eighty feet into a white-green explosion at the bottom. On the right side sits a house-sized, scooped-out rock. It has the shape of a socket. It's a tribute to the water's power.

I saw two geese at the bottom of the falls. They were on my side, waddling with necks outstretched into the woods. I bolted down the rocks (dumb), caught a leg of one as he went up the bank. He bit me on the wrist. I broke his neck.

For lunch I sautéed the heart, liver, and gizzard with a little salt, oil, and pepper. The gizzard is hard to chew unless it's cleaned of all its tissue, the leathery pouch cut away, and the muscle thinly sliced across its grain.

I made camp on the right side of the falls, just where the river curves to gather itself for the plunge. After lunch, I took the goose down to the river to pluck. My hands moved rhythmically over the body in a stroking gesture. On the upward motion I pulled feathers, first the large gray ones with the black tips. Then I plucked the next layer, the soft, white down. The wings needed another kind of attention. The wing feathers weren't fully developed. The quills were still soft, more blood than feather. They were hard to hold. There was a time when people were connected to, or at least understood, the process of killing the animals they ate. The sight of large pieces of meat and whole birds on the table was common, and acceptable.

The breeze picked up the feathers and down at my feet, lifting some out over the water. The down hovered above the river. It was hard for me to tell whether the breeze or the pull of the current was moving it. The down traveled over the water, light as a whisper, hovering or sinking on the wind. It reminded me once again that I see the wind through what it touches. I thought of Persephone, and the Greek myth about her chasing the goose into the cave and discovering the oracle of Trophonius.

The Korok is not a massive, masculine river like the Back or the Eastmain. It's womanly, with a different type of power and strength. I feel comfortable here. But then I prefer the company of women to men. I've always been more interested in what they have to say. What they choose to think about. Perhaps that comes from having three sisters. Perhaps it's the river's intimacy that intrigues me. I'm traveling from the headwaters to the mouth and I'm always able to have conversation with each bank.

I learned something last night — not to prejudge my actions. I had scouted the rapids I came through today and had convinced myself they were tougher than they actually were. Looking and responding is sometimes better than thinking and planning.

I've been rereading the first pages of this journal. I said I felt the landscape was an eternal dream, or awake in a way I hardly perceived. It's me who's been asleep. Over the past weeks I feel I've begun to accept the invitation of each day to wake up.

I'm sitting on a small hill at the bottom and to the right of the falls. I'm looking west at the mountains I'll travel between soon. The river sweeps out of sight to my right. The mountains nearest me are cut off by long, dense triangles of trees. The air is clear, cold. Everything looks flat, stacked on top of itself. The wind adds perspective by blowing clouds and their shadows up the valley. The shadows follow the contours of the mountains. The shadows seem like cloth draped over the mountains.

Today I'll just look. No thinking. No art.

And the water, sky, trees, and mountains just look back.

Evening.   Dinner: two drumsticks and rice cooked in the bird's juice with some dried apples. I have a little cold. As there wasn't much rum left, I finished it. That's given me a good buzz.

July 29.   Rest day. A wonderful, useless day. I relaxed. I made small watercolor studies of the river. I'm using pieces of the cardboard boxes the cheeses came in. The grease and wax from the cheese gives the cardboard an interesting surface to work on.

Clouds have moved in. All morning I sat by the fire and boiled the goose into soup. I was constantly feeding the fire. Showers passed. I stayed out in them. I let the rain change the watercolors. There's a chill in the air I haven't felt before.

My beard has come in full. My hands are calloused and covered with little cuts and abrasions. I cleaned my clothes. Besides the denim clothes bag, Eve made me a pullover wool shirt with a hood. It was white when I started. It's gray now, even after washing. I replaced the toggles on the hood strings with two pieces of caribou bone. I hollowed them out with my knife and carved a design in them. My underwear isn't worth much anymore. Like my pants, it could stand up on its own. I cleaned all my kitchen utensils. As I threw them back into the tray, the sound of the metal hitting metal reminded me of the daily sound of silverware being dried and thrown in the drawer at the hospital.

I walked down to gather wood from the foot of the falls. Lots of driftwood. I stopped by the lip of the falls. I sat in the heart of the noise. I stared at the water, lay right down. My head to the rock, I watched the water flow. When I looked away the rock became liquid. The landscape melted. I didn't move. I was riveted. I began playing with this sensation of looking into the water, then away. Soon the whole world melted away, or seemed to. The water's motion carried over to the landscape, making what should be stable, liquid. The sun's arc went from east to west. The weather changed from clear to cloudy, to clear and back to cloudy before I got up. All the time the water kept flowing past me. I wasn't asleep, but I wasn't awake either. What I saw I couldn't say.

I had a vivid memory of the room I grew up in. My parents' house is on a hill several miles from the ocean. It's a pink house. I had a room on the south side facing the sea. I'd lie in my bed at night watching my room change each time the Baker's Island light swept through the window. The lighthouse was far enough out to sea to make its light passing through my room a gentle one. I wouldn't notice it unless I concentrated. Sometimes I was scared by the transformations the light made because in my room I put everything in its place and it stayed there unless I moved it. On clear nights when it happened, and I was awake to see it, the beam entered every few minutes to bring alive all the mundane objects: the chair, the bureau, the closet doorknob, the pile of clothes on the floor. It changed them into fantastic shapes and silent, gliding figures. Then, in the morning, everything would be back in place. These nights were my first experience of feeling the security of a stable world changed into its opposite.

It's curious to discover childhood memories here. They form one end of a tightrope. The other end is all this around me. Between them is me, somewhere out in the middle, over the falls, balancing.

How to look at the whole of things, all the facts, not through some system's eyes or some preconceived notion? How to hold the whole picture, not just a fragment of it? How to keep it in focus and not let it boil away into some lopsided intellectual schema? How to keep it outside straight lines?

Can I? Perhaps for a second. In the seventh grade I resolved to hone my intuition to the same precision that math and science appeared to have. Knowledge was not my territory. I wanted mine to be all the formless, vague, unspecified stuff that lives before and after the facts. It's what gives facts their life. It's difficult being attracted to the inexpressible, or the less expressible, yet I can't remain speechless. To colonize that territory remains my goal. I hold suspect any "path," even my own. What I hope to find stands outside, alive, moving, changing. I've yet to find a caribou at the end of a trail. Outhouses and other dead things have paths leading to them.

July 30.   Another rest day. Two days ago, coming through the small rapids above the falls, a gust of wind blew *Monkey* sideways. I put my paddle down and let myself be blown. It would be hard to make headway against a strong wind. If I get strong head winds I'll have to wait them out.

Does July have 30 or 31 days? I can't remember the jingle. I'm saying it doesn't. I'd rather be a day ahead than behind. This afternoon I'm going to cross the river and scout the portage around the falls.

I've spent an hour trying to do a watercolor of the view from my parents' back porch. I know it like the back of my hand, but it's elusive.

There's Marblehead off to the left of the view. Out in front is Great Misery Island. Chub Island is in the foreground of the ocean. Baker's Island is on the left side. The Gooseberrys are behind Misery. The railroad tracks run parallel to the ocean's horizon. There are several large white pines that break into the scallop of ocean I can see from the porch. The distance to them might be two miles.

There's a lawn down below the porch before the hill drops off. My mother has encouraged the lawn to change over the years from the great American green lawn into a world of wildflowers. She's even transplanted wildflowers into it. Their colors are an improvement over the grass. So is the tangle of growth they shine in. But my mother's greatest horticultural achievement is her agapanthus, her Lily of the Nile. She has several she puts outside in summer. They grow in large ceramic pots. They preside on the sides of the steps going down to the lawn. The steps are gray granite, the pots are brick red, and the plants rise up from them on long, slim green stems.

For the few weeks they are in bloom, they have a starburst of unbelievable purple at their head. Just before flowering, the plant's buds are extravagant and outrageously sexual. I was attempting to point this out to my father once, when he cut me short by saying, "Yes, they're a good-looking plant."

End of the day. After lunch I paddled *Monkey* across the head of the falls. Just in from where I landed was a campsite. Maybe it was a year old. It wasn't hard to miss with all the cut trees, empty cans, shotgun shells, paper, and Day-Glo strands of rope.

Along the fall's left side is easier walking. It seems the natural portage. The first rapids below the falls are too big to shoot. I'll continue walking around the first large corner until I can see that they loosen up. I can see a passage down from there if I stay in close to shore. I'll portage everything to there, then load up and gently work my way down the rapid. A bob and weave, a back-paddle here, a glide there. I see no serious holdup.

The rapids scouted, I set up the fly rod. A hatch of mayflies had been out the last few days. I tried matching the hatch, but found my flies too small to be effective in the strong current. I changed to a big Royal Coachman streamer. I let it float downstream and sink as I stripped out line. I intended to retrieve it slowly up the eddy in front of me. I snagged something — or was it a strike? Either way it didn't hold. I made several more casts. Nothing happened. Or did it? Was that the shadow of a fish following the fly? Another cast and I hooked her. This was different. The fish spun on the surface. She, as the fish turned out to be, took me way downstream before I could land her. She was full of eggs. I had no way of carrying the roe and let the reddish-pink mass float downriver, sure it wouldn't go to waste.

This is a char! The spots on her flanks are red and orange, melting to a sunset-pink-and-orange belly, touched with whitish yellow at the throat. Her pectoral and pelvic fins are bordered with pure white and have an edging of orange and green. The jaw has an arrogant hook at the tip. She's solid muscle created for swimming, with a few fins added for balance.

Dinner was goose soup and three large char steaks. A few pancakes with honey for dessert. Eating rich protein like goose and fish, I begin to crave carbohydrates. An attitude I have on this trip different from my others is that if I desire something, I have it. If I want to stop, I do. If I want to sleep late, I enjoy it.

I spent sunset below the falls painting a watercolor of them. I let the sky and the falls remain white as if the sky fell into the falls. As the sun was giving its last licks to the mountains, I came back. I'm by the fire now, burning several large pieces of driftwood. I'm listening to the fire's crackle and the constant, thick sounds of the falls. The nights are darker now. The fire flickering seems like a blinking eye. I seem to blink in the flicker of the fire and shadows. At times, in the face of all this around me, I feel that way: sometimes there, sometimes not. My thoughts follow the flame, lick at one thing and another, dance a minute on a particular feeling before disappearing.

August 1.   After breakfast I went to say good-bye to the waterfall. I watched the water flowing a long time, enjoying it as my thought.

I opened David's fourth envelope:

When walking, just walk. When sitting, just sit.
*Above all, don't wobble.**

That's good.

What else is the water saying? What else am I being shown day by day? If I'm buckling my belt, I'm not walking. If I'm tying my boot, that's all I'm doing.

In the falls, created by the spray and brought out by the morning sun, was a small, dancing rainbow set off against the white foam.

✖

Evening. Short day. A mile-and-a-half portage. Four times around the falls for me. On the portage I shot a ptarmigan, or spruce hen, as they are called in the forest. I could hear several of them in the woods. Their call sounds like a blade being sharpened. I made a lucky shot at one sitting in the top of a tree and hit him in the head.

As I was setting up camp near where I landed the char, a dragonfly I had been watching in the air landed on my sleeve. He was a big one. The first I've seen. What I didn't notice immediately was that he had chosen my arm as the spot to finish eating the back end of a mayfly. He held the still-struggling fly down with his forelegs while his mouth sawed on the body. He ate it up to the thorax and flew off. Even after the dragonfly flew away, the front half of the mayfly continued its struggle to be free.

～

* Zen Master, Yun-Men.

151

Movies tonight. During dinner I showed the rerun of an old Samurai flick about a Master and His Apprentice. All in my head. . . . A Master teaches all he knows of swordplay, finesse, and manners to his Number-one Student. Then, the Number-one Student secludes himself on a Lonely Mountain Top to practice all the Master has taught him. He practices until he feels ready to challenge the Master to a duel. The only way for him to become a Master.

He invites himself to dinner. During conversation over their fish and rice, the Master calmly picks flies out of the air with his chopsticks. This disconcerts the Young Samurai, who reconsiders his challenge. He returns to his Lonely Mountain Top until he, too, can pluck flies from the air with his chopsticks. Then he challenges the Master. His challenge is accepted.

They meet on the appointed day. They stand at the appropriate distance on the dueling ground. The shadows from their hats obscure their eyes. They close slowly in the traditional way. Rather, the Young One advances. The Old Master stands casually, hands in his sleeves. Closer, closer the Young One advances until he's within striking distance. His sword is raised, but he hesitates. He's puzzled at the Old Master's nonchalance. He begins his first swing. Now the Master moves. He takes his hands out of his sleeves. His right hand holds a .45 pistol. He drops the Apprentice in mid-swing. . . . Hah! And remains Master.

❧

August 2. I didn't run a second feature. The wind came up from the southeast, the one direction my tent was not protected from. I waited, watching those same dark gray, swirling, sinuous clouds that I'd watched all night in the

Palmer Valley. They tumbled and poured themselves across the sky. They were rushing toward the Atlantic. At the same time, beside me the black river ran to Ungava Bay, full of its own swirling, tumbling current-self. I sensed the huge contradiction of currents and eddies and surfaces in me. I felt in harmony with that black weather. I was scared.

I built a windscreen. The simpler solution would have been to move the tent. Instead, I cut small spruces and leaned them against the canoe. I'd placed *Monkey* lengthwise along the backside of the tent. I leaned the tops of the spruces toward the tent. I kept piling them there until I had protected my home. I laid a large log across their bottoms and brought the biggest rocks I could up from the river to hold the log down. The trees would diffuse a strong wind.

I kept adding another spruce here, a rock there, thinking I'd best be ready for the worst. I had to stop when it got too dark to see. I crossed my fingers and went to bed. I feared I wouldn't get much sleep, but I did.

The worst that happened is that it rained, but all morning the woods seemed to be holding a little of last night's blackness in their branches, a residue I can feel in myself, too.

I've been taking pictures of my elaborate windscreen, the tent, my fireplace, and the rock lichens. Today I'll stay put, fix the tumpline, sew the hole in my shirt, and sharpen my ax and knife.

Evening. In the afternoon I take a walk away from the river. Without *Monkey* on my back, or the gun, or a heavy load, I move quickly. I feel light as the wind ambling in and out of the treeline. I spook an old bull caribou. In his retreat, he seems to dance away from me, tilting his great rack up and down as he runs.

August 3. Overcast. Left camp expecting to portage around rapids marked on the map, but I found a way through. I scared five large trout in the shallow water at its head.

The morning continued as a series of ripples, or short rapids. Whenever I came across fast water, I either stopped to fish or cast from *Monkey* as I floated by. I caught several lightweight trout in the big back-eddies just after the rapids. I came to a narrows where the river was forced in between two ledges. One ledge hung out over the river. It began to rain.

There's nothing quieter than a light rain. As the gray sky deepens, the river darkens. A ring appears where each droplet hits the water. Because of the immense number of drops that begin falling, I expect to hear a sound. I never do. The dark water brushing up against the rock ledge makes white lines, shimmering white lines like a silk cloth moving in night light. At the bottom of the rapid, drifting through the bubbles caused by the agitated water, I notice that the larger bubbles reflect me and the canoe. They distort us as though I am looking in a convex mirror.

By lunch I reached the Grenier River. It was inviting. I camped under a tall tamarack that had been struck by lightning. There's a beach in front of me and a huge pool in front of that where the Grenier feeds into the Korok. I caught

Lower Korok River

154

lunch on a fly. I put the trout on a spit and ate the meat off as it cooked.

I experimented fishing the deep pool in different ways. I tried flies, both dry and wet, streamers, and a small spinner. Each caught fish, which I set free, but what attracted the most followers was a large Dardevle reeled in slowly. I kept four trout for dinner.

I had a memory of catching my first trout. On Cape Cod, my father and I were fishing several ponds run by a man named Tuttle. I must have been all of six years old. I didn't know how to fly-fish. I got bored trying to learn. When my father wasn't looking, or I thought he wasn't, I'd fish for the small, freshly stocked trout swimming back and forth in front of the stone dam. I actually caught one by jiggling a bumble-bee fly in front of its nose. I don't know who was more surprised, me, the fish, or my father.

I've just spent several hours cutting and splitting firewood. What a pleasure not to have to spend hours gathering willow twigs! I saw black bear tracks down the beach.

I'm in a rhythm now.

August 4.   Windy day. Cold. The morning has the feeling of alabaster. Down came the wind, locking me in for the day. Fine with me. Cut more firewood. Look a lot. Go down to the pool and catch a trout to have with my pancakes. Then catch one for lunch. That's where we are now, lunch.

8.4.79
Dear Mr. McIlhenny,
    I noticed your address on my bottle of Tabasco and I just wanted to say your sauce is great. Although if you're part of the family responsible for the extinction of the ivory-billed wood-

*pecker on Avery Island, you ought to be shot. Keep to the sauce.
The hotter, the better.*

Sincerely,

Rob Perkins

Korok River, Northern Labrador.

My first fan letter!
The mountain slopes sit perpendicular to the horizontal
line of the pine trees. The deep green in the pine forest near
the river melts into the lighter green of the moss higher up
where the tundra begins. Patches of dark green are scattered
high up, indicating where there was sufficient shelter for a
few trees to grow.

Took a nap this afternoon. On the moss. Don't know how
long I slept. No idea what time it is. If I didn't keep the
journal I wouldn't know what day it is. What I do know is
that it is now dinner time.

August 5.   Had to get up in the night to pee. Outside, an
unexpected pleasure: the Northern Lights. A sky-bound,
silent-river waterfall. They fitted my half-asleep mood. They
were slow-motion swirls, swinging back and forth, bunching
up, unwinding. They were creating a beautiful slow dance
across the blackness. It was similar to seeing a flock of small
migrating birds; their bodies fold and unfold in space, from
dots to a solid mass, each time they change direction. The
difference between them is that the Northern Lights move
much, much more slowly across a universe of space.

Pancakes for breakfast and a look at the map. I've one full
week before meeting Richard. Five days of travel if I want to

arrive two days before he is flown in. There are a few portages and thirty miles between here and the island. I'll take another day off.

I've spotted a group of river beauties to work into a water-color. The day is gray and cold. Fall's coming. The crowberry and blueberry leaves are beginning to turn red. The gray weather and cold wind make the river beauties appear more delicate and colorful. Their pink color is offset by black rock. I did several studies of them, but couldn't satisfy myself. One was coming close but I ruined it. In disgust I went to saw and split wood. I nicked the ax but good because I was working fast and angrily.

I went hunting. I was more interested in walking and look-ing than in shooting. I found a group of *white* river beauties. It's the first white example I've ever seen of *Epilobium lati-folium*.

I forgot about hunting and put eyes on my feet. For most of the afternoon I kept my head close to the ground. What I discovered was an army of spiders, each one fortified in its own little bunker. First I noticed the white cottony web of one. Soon I saw them all around me. Each web was cone-shaped, with the point of the white cone ending at a black hole where the spider hid. The architecture was delicate, a mixture of overlaid webbing. Each one had its own curious shape according to whatever configuration of twigs or leaves was acting as the support. Even my slightest move sent the spider scurrying into its hole, but if I held my breath and kept my shadow from falling on them I was the voyeur of a strange world.

They play a waiting game. What are they doing while they wait? When they move, their legs spring them forward like oars. For their big bodies and thick, hairy legs, they hardly shake their web. Watching them didn't improve my meal supply for the next week, however.

Coming back to camp, walking along the shore, written in the sand, I saw today's *Tundra Times* headline: MOTHER AND BABY CARIBOU FOLLOWED BY WOLF.

Split-pea soup tonight, Tabasco, and plenty of garnish. When I write my tundra cookbook it will have this heading under garnishes: "In addition to the more substantial foods like fish, game, and wild vegetables, the tundra provides garnishes in two sizes.

"Taste varies according to amount of garnish used, but one can be sure a mixture of blackflies and mosquitoes is available for every meal. For hot dishes, such as soups, either leave the pot uncovered, or set the individual servings aside until the desired amount of garnish appears on top. For cold dishes the garnish can be obtained with a slap on an exposed forearm."

In George Back's journal he tells how Sir John Franklin never killed an insect, but brushed it off with a loving pat. Back didn't say whether he thought it a peculiar habit, or if he practiced it himself, but I could never do it. I hate blackflies and I hate mosquitoes, especially when one gets caught in my ear. They're all my bad thoughts coming to get me. They're terrible. Every night, after closing the tent, I can't sleep until I've killed them all. The straightforward slap is too good for them. There are many varieties of hand rolls, thumb pokes, knuckle punches, and pinches to be practiced on the little darlings.

August 6.   Didn't rise early. Stayed in bed thinking, listening to the wind and intermittent rain sweep over the tent.

This is the anniversary of the day the atom bomb was dropped on Hiroshima. For a peace-loving nation, we're the only one to have dropped an atom bomb on people.

When I did get up, I had one trout and some fried rice for breakfast. I rolled up. The clouds were low but the weather had lightened.

Leaving the campsight, I looked back a last time. When everything is in the canoe and I'm ready to leave, I make one more check to be sure I have everything. I had to chuckle. The beach looked like the Chinese army had passed through, instead of one person. In the last two days I've left hundreds of footprints headed all directions. But in a day or two my presence will be washed and blown away.

I had to choose which side of an island to go down. I chose the left. I tend to favor the left, the moon's side, the silver side, the intuitive side. I stayed in tight to shore to avoid the tall standing waves in the middle. A small three-foot fall ended the set, but by sliding in on the far corner and giving two powerful strokes, I slid by into the eddy and ran down another hundred yards. Then I portaged to avoid a steeper six-foot fall.

As the river widened, a head wind began blowing. I pulled into the lee of a point and pitched a fly. It's great to have trees to pitch to. The rain came, but I was dry under the fly, sitting on the wannigan, with a small fire in front of me.

The weather cleared, or began to. I took a few casts into the small rapid in front of me and raised a trout. This was his territory, but he soon was caught. I ate him with the remainder of the pea soup. Johnny May's plane flew over very high, headed upriver. I wished I were just beginning again.

I continued an hour through a landscape of rolling mountains, streams entering, and gullies. They were all inviting me to stop and wander. According to the map, I was getting close to the island. I began thinking of ways to slow down. I told myself this was so I wouldn't have to spend a week in one place, but it's really because the island marks the end of my solo trip.

I've come to where I can see a waterfall coming down the mountains to my right. It reminds me of the ones in the Palmer Valley, except it's miles from the river. I can't hear it. I barely perceive its movement. It's like a memory, or a dream, not like the ones in the Palmer Valley at all. I decided to camp.

Johnny's plane flew back downriver, a peppercorn in the sky. I wonder what business he had on the Atlantic side? The blackflies are bad. Rain. I'm sitting in the tent to get away from both. Feel sad. I'm listening to the monotonous sound of rain on the tent.

Evening.   Must have dozed, because I jumped when I heard a peculiar bird. Couldn't quite place the high-pitched whistle of its call. I crawled out of the tent, into sunshine.

I get the gun. Not to hunt the bird, but as an excuse to go into the woods. That funny depression is with me again. I scramble up the knoll behind the tent. Halfway up it, I realize my sounds are being mirrored by ones receding down the opposite side. I find the tracks of a bear on top. I wait until the sounds end before entering the trees. At first I move slowly, tentatively. I feel apprehensive, not about the bear as much as about my mood. I'm listening. I begin to amble in an unfocused way. I travel deeper and deeper into the woods' silence. The farther I go, the more tangled and overgrown the forest becomes. The softer it is underfoot. Then I begin moving faster. I realize I'm not hunting. I have no intention of it. I am heading for the waterfall.

I sidestep, duck, and push through tightly packed spruces. The blackflies are fierce. I follow game trails when I can. Still inside the forest, I begin to climb uphill. I can't see the waterfall, but I can hear it now. The trees begin to thin out. Then I hear that queer birdcall again. I can't see it, or place its eerie call.

I climb out onto the large, white boulders of the waterfall's riverbed. I leave the trees. The fall is still some distance away and I begin to climb.

A peregrine falcon dive-bombs me. It was his high, piercing twitter I had heard. Almost a whistle. From now on I lose sight of him, but I can hear his cry. As I reach the fall its roar drowns out all but its own sound.

It's too sharp a climb to the top. Instead I stand under the fall's steepest drop. The falling water cools the air around itself. Looking straight up, there is only blue sky above the white, boiling water pouring over the rock lip. The wetness illuminates the fool's gold flecked throughout the rocks. The beads of water glitter as they break. The main fall is a crashing white torrent, smashing into the pool at the bottom. Like a deep breath, the pool catches the fall. I stay as long as the blackflies allow me.

I've decided not to dawdle, but to move on to the island. Something good will happen then. Dragging my heels is no good. It's wobbling.

At dinner I made my first deep-fried quoits. A quoit is a curious beast. It's a cross between a fritter and a doughnut. I mix a regular biscuit dough, but instead of baking it, I flatten a small ball of it in my hand. Then with my ring I press a hole in it. I submerge it in boiling grease. I push a stick with a forking branch into the ground near the fire. Using another stick to fish out the quoits, I ring them up on the first stick. This keeps them warm while I cook the rest.

I ate them while the sun diffused its last light through thin veils of clouds passing overhead. This created rainbow after rainbow. Eating my quoits in this sublime watercolor made me a happy man.

August 7.   After breakfast, after packing up, I opened David's second-to-last letter. If I were a nail and that letter a hammer, it hit me square on the head:

> *When lightning flashes, how admirable is he who thinks not, "Life is fleeting."**

Paddle in the morning. No wind. Being on the river is riding liquid glass. I can see down to the bottom, which is over my head, but doesn't look it.

In the middle of the morning, a group of geese flew up, splashing off the left bank. I went to see if one or two hadn't decided to hide. Some had. Before realizing what I was shooting, I fired and hit a gosling. Another gosling took to the water with its parents. From the middle of the river they faced the shore and called to their child. I chased the wounded gosling until I caught him. His feathers were just

* Haiku Poet, Bashō

coming in. They would have been his first plumage. He looked scrawny and pathetic lying at my feet, but not as pathetic as I felt for having killed him.

Killing is murder. Hunting and fishing aren't sport. They're not. All my life I've done both without question.

My father bought me a BB gun when I was thirteen. I hunted. After weeks of trying I killed my first chickadee. I can still see the bird hanging upside down from the branch of a pine tree, intent on its feeding. This time the BB didn't miss. The bird jumped, let go its hold, and fell. I was scared. I didn't know what to do now that I'd killed it. The woods seemed to grow quieter. My heart's sound, my breathing, and my guilt grew louder in contrast. In my hand the bird had no weight. Its coloring was black and white and gray. I imagined the small brass ball pushing through the feathers, entering the body, cracking a bone, stopping. I buried it under pine needles. I can still smell the acid aroma of those needles. I cried.

When I was older I went on a deer hunt. It was on an island off the coast of Massachusetts. In the winter the deer would starve if their numbers weren't controlled. Anyway, that was the justification. Nobody dwelled on the fact that their habitat had been taken over by people. That people had killed off their natural enemies. That the organization of life no longer happened, but had to be controlled by people.

There was a light snow. I was put in a clearing of apple trees. I held a double-barreled shotgun with two loads of buckshot. Half the hunters were driving the deer, the other half waiting as I was. Two deer bounded into the clearing; I shot one. It didn't fall right away. I ran after it. Red blood on the snow brought me to where the deer had collapsed a hundred yards into the woods. One of the men remarked it was a lung shot, which takes longer to kill.

A sport is competition between consenting adversaries. Animals and fish don't consent, which makes it something else.

Only today, standing over the gosling, did I recognize one of my feelings from the day I shot the deer. I had no pride in what I'd done. Something alive was dead. I had murdered.

Two hours' paddle brought me to the rapids before the island. This one was a mile of white water dropping around two corners. There were lots of rocks. If I took it slowly down the edge and kept close to shore, I would have no problems. It was crowded with plenty of tight turns, backups, crossovers, and at the bottom it opened up, gaining a lot of power. Big swells, few rocks. I kept telling myself to treat it the same as any other rapid. But I knew it was the last rapid *Monkey* and I would shoot alone. I wanted to open up. I wanted to ride right down the middle, down the simplest and most direct route, to travel through the largest swells and risk turning over for the sheer pleasure of the last ride.

After scouting the rapid, I carried this dialogue on all the way back to *Monkey*. I knew I shouldn't take risks. The privilege was being here, not shooting the toughest water like a kayaker.

I looked at *Monkey*. I edged the canoe into the current.

We shot the rapid right down the middle — bang.

The island was a mile farther downstream. I found a good campsite near the west end.

I'm looking across the river to the mountains set far back from the opposite shore. Those silent mountains, this quiet river. That's what it's all about.

No, those silent mountains, this quiet river: that's what I'm about.

August 8.   I stayed in bed late, enjoying the feeling of having made it. Also, I stayed in the tent to avoid facing the blackflies and mosquitoes. Yesterday, I had to build two smudge fires when I landed. Their smoke helped keep the bugs at bay.

I wonder what it will be like to talk to someone. I wonder what Richard's like.

Evening.   It was cold when I got up. I put on a pair of light socks and a pair of heavier socks over them. I wore my rain pants over my khaki pants. I put on a T-shirt, a wool shirt, my wool pullover, and my parka.

Late in the afternoon I went to look at the rapids below camp. I beached *Monkey* at their head and followed the tracks of a bear down to the fast water. I tried the fly rod, then a few casts with the spinning rod. Nothing. I kept walking down, fishing the back-eddies that looked interesting.

I could see a small four-foot fall farther down. Those huge, flat-made-smooth-by-the-water rocks that mark large drops in the river. I felt pretty sure there'd be trout there. I stood a long time admiring the small fall, the solid curve of water falling into a frothy, swirling eddy. On my side near the head of the eddy, there was a piece of clear water. It was deep. I jigged a Dardevle in it. Nothing.

Until my fifth try.

Then I had a strike, but I couldn't hook him. The Dardevle I was using has only one hook because it carries easier in my pocket. The problem is that it doesn't hook a fish easily. I finally hooked one. I had him on the rocks when he threw the hook, flip-flopped back into the water. This wasn't a trout. It was a beautiful, silver star straight from the ocean. I yelled out loud for the first time in days. "Char."

Then I began noticing the dark shapes of other fish. I saw one jump up the side of the fall. I walked to the edge, peered over into the pool by the head of the fall. The pool wasn't large, but it was full of char, their heads lower than their tails. They lay there waiting for their moment to leap the falls. Huge ones, little ones, their silver color appearing green and gunmetal blue in the water. I put my hand in the pool to touch them. If I was fast I could brush their tails as they sank out of reach. Their tails felt like fans. This was their upriver spawning run.

I moved below the fall into the rapids, where I could cast. I wanted to catch one on a fly. I could see them now. They were surfacing everywhere. Two there, one there, five together over there. Hundreds of them. I cast and cast, changed flies, fished slower, fished fast. I would get strikes, but could not hook one.

It began to get late. The cold day turned from blue to dark blue to purple. I was fishing into the molten reflection of the setting sun on the water. I began to ache.

The wind dropped. The blackflies appeared in droves. I walked all the way down the rapids. No luck. At the foot of

Char

168

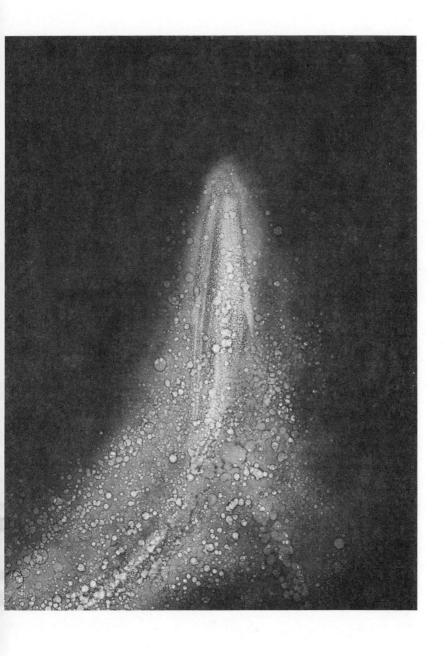

the rapid, in a large pool, I saw a grandfather char drifting in the eddy. His movements were S-curve undulations. He sat there four feet in front of me and six feet deep. I couldn't interest him in anything. I even cheated and put a tiny Dardevle on my fly rod. He could have cared less. I felt like breaking the rod over my knee and throwing it at him.

The sun set. I came back below the falls. I put on a Coachman streamer. I gave it a good cast at right angles to the current. Stripping in the belly of the line, I began to retrieve the fly, but it snagged a rock. I was so pissed. I yanked it. I couldn't free it. Exasperated, I decided to break the leader and call it a day. I jerked hard several times, really hard. It jerked back! Unbelievable. I had hooked one. A big one.

He took off. I found out what having a hundred yards of backing on my reel meant. I ran downstream along the shore. I ran through the water, over rocks, trying to keep up. I knew if I tried to check his run I'd lose all my line. I wondered what I was supposed to do. He kept going. The first joints of my fingers ached from the reel handle knocking them as the fish spun off more and more line.

He slowed down. I gained back a little line. Soon, I had my backing on the reel. The sky was dark now. The wind had gone. The blackflies were eating me alive. I could do nothing about it. My full attention was with the fish, who sat at the bottom of a pool fifty feet offshore. I waited an hour. All the time I felt the fish was in control, not me. I couldn't put any bug dope on or even swat the bastard flies. I had to keep both hands on the rod, applying a subtle pressure.

It was dark walking back to the canoe with the fish. The gleam of the white in the rocks, the white of the fish's belly, and the glint of the silver ring on my left hand were all I could see. The rest of the world was dark. Then the August moon rose, white with an orange halo. It appeared slowly over the black mountains.

I cooked a large steak by firelight and went to bed.

August 9.   Richard arrived early. He told me it's really the eighth. It figures: a month named after Julius Caesar would be a *big* month.

August 10.   Yesterday when the plane buzzed my camp, I didn't realize it was bringing Richard. I didn't know quite what they were doing. It turned out the pilot hadn't trusted the depth of water in front of me. He didn't dare land there. Hearing the roar of the engines a little later, I realized they had landed downriver and dropped Richard, or something, off.

Too excited to think, I ran to *Monkey*. I beached the canoe at the head of the rapids. I ran down the rocks. I slipped, twisted my ankle slightly, laughed, and hobble-hopped on. I saw Richard. He was moving unsteadily over the rocks with his duffle on his shoulder. Swearing, sweating, he stopped to wait for me.

Meeting, we embraced. I couldn't speak. He handed me a plum! A plum. I couldn't believe I was biting into a plum. A juicy, soft, wet plum.

Richard was having a terrible time with the bugs. Sweat fogged his glasses. He smelled sweet, civilized. They loved him. We laughed. I shared carrying his load back to *Monkey*.

Before I could introduce him to *Monkey*, Richard said, "That's a nice-looking canoe."

He said it. My stomach sank. How could I explain *Monkey*

was my friend? My companion? And not just "a nice-looking canoe"?

Two people felt different in *Monkey*. I hadn't thought to bring a paddle from camp for Richard. He sat on the bottom of the canoe facing me. I hadn't had someone look at me in a while. It was strange. I couldn't look at him.

The day's light rain was clearing. A great arc of rainbow appeared upriver. There was dark sky behind it. The mountains off to the right were caught and melted in the long, oblique sunlight — melted into sharp contrasts of gold and black shadows. The rainbow seemed a revealed arc, one I'd passed through and wouldn't . . .

Click, click, click, Richard was shooting, *click*. Something in his manner, in the noise of that shutter, I didn't like. *Click*. One rainbow down on film. He turned back toward me. He asked me to keep paddling. I didn't know where to look. I couldn't avoid him or his camera.

At camp I cooked him a char steak and heated up the goose soup. Richard found the soup bland, and took his turn to cook me a char steak the way he liked them, smothered in sauce. He said he didn't like fish that much, but his special sauce improved its taste.

He spread out an array of goodies. Eggs, sausage, poppy-seed bread, butter. I almost ate breakfast right after dinner. With effort, I resisted. I slept badly. I tossed and turned all night.

✖

August 11.   Talking is exhausting. I feel more comfortable writing in the journal. Richard won't stop asking me questions. My answers don't sound right. I'm very dissatisfied with words, mine and his.

But eggs!!! That's another story. We cooked a breakfast of fried eggs, sausage, and poppy-seed bread with butter!

We went to pick up the extra food he'd left where the plane landed. Walking with someone felt strange. I wanted his company, but felt distracted by it. What was familiar to me was new to him. He photographed everything.

The ground cover and woods were wet. Before long we were soaked. We cut through the forest to walk in the tundra. On the plateau we saw a caribou. *Click, click, click,* Richard was off stalking him. The caribou was as amused as I was watching Richard sneak toward him on his belly. The caribou left when he felt like it, and Richard, when he got back to me, said, "Did you see that? Did you see that? I got really close to him."

The food duffle was tied into a dead tree. Richard said this was to protect it from the bears. It took us ten minutes to untie the Gordian knot Richard had created to secure it. We laughed and agreed the knots would've slowed a bear down, too.

On the way back, we walked near the river. We see different things in the landscape. Now I have two other eyes to see the land through, and to see myself.

I think I'll go cut some wood.

August 12.   Rain most of the night. We woke to find the river had risen four feet. Combined with yesterday's rain, that makes eight to ten feet in two days.

We abandoned the first fireplace and built one under the fly, up against the bank.

More eggs and sausage for breakfast. Today, we had home-baked yeast bread.

Richard says he wants to spend two weeks out here. I don't. With the rain, there's not a lot to do. I feel comfortable doing nothing. Richard doesn't. Across the river are high clay banks, then forest, and towering over the trees, the mountains framing that side of the valley. Halfway up the cliff of one of the mountains is a huge, pyramid-shaped white rock. Richard believes it's magical. That someone put it there for a reason. He keeps suggesting we climb up to it.

August 13.   Richard asked me to help him build a blind so he can lie in wait to photograph caribou. I declined.

He is an EST graduate. He's been feeling me out about my beliefs. He even brought a book for me to read about it.

August 13

Dear Mandy,

How good those words sound to me. Who knows when you'll read this, or where, but now, right now, we're both still in the thick of our dreams. I can't imagine what Rome is like.

Rome . . . Rome . . . Rome. I say the word and I see history, man's will, art, law, order, Catullus, debauchery, Fellini, bread, cheese, wine, workmen in blue overalls spraying down early morning streets, architecture, balance, symmetry, capuccino, sandals, shorts (two things I never wear), all those white Brooklyn Romans in the '50s Hollywood movies, their one greasy lock pasted to their forehead, vegetables, fish on ice, crowds, catacombs, walls, churches, St. Peter's key hole, ruins . . . and the little dot with the circle around it in my atlas when I was thirteen looking at Europe. The circle around the dot meant a lot of people lived there. Rome couldn't be more different from where I am.

I'm sitting under my tarp, enjoying the feeling of a full stomach.

I'm having a cup of tea. It's evening. I'm a happy man but what I wouldn't give to have one of those frozen, hollowed-out lemons with lemon sherbet inside it. After handing me the stainless-steel holder on a small plate with a small spoon to eat it with, a smiling, dark-haired girl in white would give me a napkin and I'd take all to a small, marble table. And it would be hot in the street. And I'd put my hand on the cool marble. Before I began to eat, I'd smile because there were no mosquitos, no blackflies, but you sitting across from me.

And I must tell you I've had an incredible journey. So full of joy and wonder and speechlessness. Full days, full stomachs, short days, hungry ones, painful ones, hours and hours spent just looking, walking in the mountains, my spirit with the highest peaks, moments when I was afraid for my life, quiet moments, moments when everything in the world made sense, others when I was down, so down. In other words, normal days. Normal, except each day here has an intensity to it. I'm a flame here, not the ember I am at home. Home? I feel more comfortable here than I ever have anywhere.

Richard the photographer has joined me. Do you remember talking about that? How you told me not to bother about feeling obliged to the magazines? I wish I had listened. The fire in front of me is more companionable than he is. It's not his fault. It's just that after weeks alone it's hard sharing myself and this experience with someone so different.

Your wrist band reached me before I left. It has guided me since the first day. It has made me happy to look at it and think of you. I wonder what you're doing today?

It rained here. We moved the fire to the edge of the tarp, cut lots of wood, and have enjoyed a warm, dry day under it, with no bugs.

My pink flamingo is looking at me. Did I tell you about him? I decided for my home this summer to bring something attractive for the front yard. So I brought the flamingo.

*How can I tell you about my trip? I can't. I've had moments
of clarity, though. Coming back along a portage trail, having
taken one load across, or two, I would stop and stand still. My
neck and shoulders would be uncoiling from the weight of the
load. I'd see the tundra better. Not that my sight was clearer, but
my mind was less cluttered. What I saw entered my brain more
directly, filled it completely, like moments when we make love.*

*I've felt my ideas about nature changing. I came believing how
sliding, changeable, and multiple she was. In a way she is: slight
shifts of light, or a breath of wind changes forever what just was.
The days don't repeat. However, she endures in a more distant
way, a cold way. The light, the wind, the water, the sky, they
abide. They have a subtle, lasting rhythm we don't feel as often.
We have a sparrow's sight and call the world changing, ever
changing. Yet, caught in tonight's brief sunset, I didn't find myself
filled with thoughts of the eternal. I saw the sun set below a low
bank of clouds. That's all. I watched a very particular, beautiful
thing happen and felt the tension, the balance between the
particular and the forever of longer rhythms.*

*A wave of emotion swept over me, a premonition, a black one,
about how utterly capable we are of destroying ourselves and the
earth. How incapable we are of learning from our past experiences,
how engulfed we are in technology, in old industrial ways of
thinking, and how self-centered we are about the earth as long
as we have our little piece of it.*

*What's made the trip unique are the waterfalls. I knew what
one was before I came here, but for the first two weeks each
feeder stream into the river I was climbing up was a waterfall.
They'd rivet me. They were white lines connecting heaven to
earth, except one. I found a small one. Rather I found a place
where a small one used to flow. It's trail remained, a black line
down the rocks. A silent, black waterfall. I remembered it tonight
when I had my premonition.*

Mandy, let's not let anything bad happen to us. My heart aches to see you. I'll be so nervous when we meet. I wonder if you'll be able to tell. I try not to live in the past with you, but our present ended the morning you stepped on the train. I hope we are able to see through the images we have of each other to what we are when we meet. It's effortless loving you, thinking about you.

Rob

August 14–16.

August 17. Hmmmmmm. I haven't kept up with the journal since Richard arrived. He's been with me nine days. We've moved at a leisurely pace over the last thirty miles of the river. *Monkey* barely holds us both and all our gear.

Richard would like to shoot every rapid and looks at me as though I am an amateur when I say no, not until we're used to each other in the canoe. Not to mention that a lot of the water we portage around is unshootable anyway.

It's raining again. We're sitting under the fly, looking at two pretty waterfalls across the river. I've been doing some chores: fixing my belt, whipping back together the two pieces of the leather loop that hold the buckle. I've darned a hole in my woolen pullover.

I can hear the rapids we portaged around yesterday off to my right. There's a sand beach in front of us. We put the tent up on the bank on a soft bed of moss. I baked a yeast bread in the frying pan to have with our tea. Richard doesn't drink tea. He says it's too strong a stimulant.

Having him join me has made for an entirely different trip.

It's an injury. So far he's lost a number of lures, hit rocks with the ax, and used up half a roll of toilet paper starting fires. He's trying to be helpful and doesn't understand why I get restive.

On our walk yesterday we saw a seagull scavenging on the river. Richard preferred to call it the "mysterious white bird." I didn't argue.

This a.m., having eaten all our char, we went to catch more. We caught three. Richard caught his first fish ever. That was very exciting for him and pleased me. It was as large as the first large one I caught on the fly rod. It took off downstream and Richard landed it and left it to pick up later. Almost immediately after Richard left, the "mysterious white bird" started to peck out its eyes. That made me furious. Yell as loud as I could, the bird wouldn't leave until I went back for the fish. Reluctantly, Richard admitted, perhaps, it might be a seagull.

Tonight we saw a bear! A thin sow. She was working the side of the river at dusk, a large black shape moving over the light-colored rocks. Her head was weaving from side to side. We had been trolling from the canoe and were able to glide close to her, but in three bounds she was off the rocks and into the woods, graceful and fast.

Since Richard's come I've hurt myself twice. The afternoon he arrived, on my way to meet him, and the first day we went fishing. The day he arrived I was so excited, I was running on wet rocks. I slipped and turned my ankle, not badly, but it was the first time this summer. The other time was a day or two after he arrived. We were fishing. The water had risen, preventing us from easily reaching the small falls I wanted to fish. I jumped a gap between two rocks, from a high one to a low one, not pausing to consider how I'd get back. Richard didn't join me. He even pointed out I might have difficulty getting back before I jumped. I did. My running broad jump got me half on the higher rock, while my thighs, particularly my left one, slammed into the rock. I could barely walk that evening. We had talked about climbing the mountain across from us the next day — to investigate that magical white rock. The next morning I was in pain and sullen. I didn't want to go, but Richard insisted.

I was glad he did. The walking felt good. It loosened up my thigh. From on top, the view down the valley and of the river brought out a whole other world. Fall is coming; browns, reds, gold have overtaken the landscape. Richard took some close-up pictures of several caribou we surprised. I did some watercolors. Being that high and surrounded by rocks again and finding a pure black lake at the top, the source of a small waterfall, made the day a gem. The magical white rock seemed to be just a rock, although Richard kept circling it looking for its larger significance.

Now a lot of my energy goes into eating. I'm always hungry.

✂

August 19.   Last night we camped on low, hard river bottom. The landscape has flattened out. Although a quarter to a half mile wide, the Korok is very shallow. All day we had to look for the main channel through the sandbars.

Today we should reach the end of the river. If the Inuit fishing camp is still open, we might get a ride with them to George River. If not, then we'll paddle sixty miles of Ungava

180

Bay to the settlement. I don't like the idea. *Monkey* is too small for us to be on the ocean.

Evening. We packed up in the morning under a gray sky. The water was calm, smooth except where a sandbar or a rock disturbed the current. We paddled several miles to the last rapid marked on the map. The portage around the top of the rapid was a well-worn trail, full of cut trees and broken branches. The rapid drained into a large, deep bend in the river, the bend we thought the Inuit camp would be in. Describing to me where the camp was, Kingsbury Browne put his thumb down on the map saying, "Look for the camp there." Well, Kingsbury, that's a big thumb you've got.

Richard insisted we shoot the last part of the rapid. He hadn't shot many and this would be his last chance. I was not as eager. It was long and complicated. I didn't want to take chances. The white water hid several rocks. Our course would have a lot of zigs and zags and sideways moves, a difficult shoot even if the two people knew how to work together. We carried the heavy loads to the end, went back, and shot the rapid. We hit a few rocks, bruising *Monkey*. That made me mad. We took some water, too. We got angry at each other, then retreated into silence, each blaming the other for our awkward descent. We emptied the canoe, loaded the gear back in, and paddled onto the open water as the sun came out.

We couldn't find the camp. I'd think it was over there. Richard would automatically point to the opposite shore. When neither case proved right, the thought that we'd be paddling the sixty miles down the coast became more real.

Two of us and the equipment in a fourteen-and-a-half-foot canoe on the open bay, traveling a barren coastline with forty-foot tides, didn't appeal to either of us.

The wind came up. On this large piece of water it created high waves. We were locked in. We were upset. We worked on each other. Richard was sure we were stranded. He watched me open the wannigan to get out the last of the cheese and nuts. He got mad and said we should save them. I ignored him. We yelled, letting out our resentment toward each other and our situation. We sullenly shared several handfuls of food. Although it didn't solve the problem, it gave us something to do. Richard climbed a ridge and came back to say he saw nothing like a cabin ahead of us. We apologized. I said how hard it must have been for him to join me. We discussed the situation. Then left the bend paddling down the last, wide miles of the Korok.

First we heard the motor.

Looking ahead, the small dark shape of a freighter canoe detached itself from the landscape. It swung downriver, disappeared. Hearing the motor dissolved my worry, but created another.

As we paddled closer the shape of a cabin, a real cabin, not the imaginary ones of an hour before, appeared in the landscape. Its color was the same gray of the rocks, the tar paper the same black. Its shape, its lines made it seem out of place.

My editor says that if artists could spell, they wouldn't be artists.

BLESS THE HUMBLE QUIOT

I stopped paddling to marvel at it. Questioningly, Richard turned to look at me.

A cabin. There it was. The end. Sitting on a ledge above the river. I imagined the Inuit's surprise. We paddled quickly to the rocks below the ledge it was built on. A child's round face appeared in the window. The face looked down at us. A woman appeared behind the child. Both disappeared.

Richard and I could hardly move fast enough up the rocks. I slowed down in front of the cabin and followed Richard inside.

The cabin was hot. There were cooked pies on top of the oven. More pie dough was rolled out on the table. The smells were warm, rich, and overwhelming.

The woman was too shy to talk to us. The child hid behind her legs. As much as the heat, and feeling and seeing the woman and her child, their softness, and the abundant smells, it was noticing three large frying pans hanging on the wall that made me smile. I couldn't stop smiling. Their big round shapes with the long handles, hung side by side, dark against the lighter wall, told me I was done.

Richard went on and on and on about how we needed to get to George River and could we stay with them and could we buy some flour, and where was her husband. At each additional question the woman's smile grew larger. Richard wasn't pausing to let her answer, but I felt she didn't care, or understand what he was saying.

I was glad to stand behind Richard, quiet, looking, aware of being in a house, in a home, near a woman.

EPILOGUE

June 12, 1982.   Written waiting for the subway to Central Park to join the march against nuclear arms.

This morning, searching for something else, I opened a drawer and discovered an insignificant-looking piece of rock covered with light-green and black lichen. Another person would have passed it over or thrown it out, but I recognized a small piece of the tundra. I picked the rock up the day I left Fort Chimo for Boston.

It was snowing the August day I flew out. Richard had left a week ahead of me. A cold wind hammered along the dirt streets as I went to several Inuit houses, hoping to buy some frozen salmon. I bought several good-sized fish for under a dollar a pound.

My flight left at twelve noon. In the air, the weather was clear and looked cold as we crossed northern Quebec toward Montreal. There were only three other passengers in the plane, two Inuit and their daughter. The little girl was sick and they were taking her to the large city hospital.

I had only ten minutes in the Montreal airport to make my connection with the day's last shuttle to Boston. This second plane was crowded, and during the flight my beard began to itch, my wool shirt became too hot, and my muscles throbbed from the inactivity of the last week. I began to feel sour and it didn't help my mood to notice how soft the people around me looked, and how sweet they smelled.

As we circled Boston, I brightened and realized, looking out the window, that it was a hot, late-summer afternoon down below. I could see the halo of haze around the city. There were the white dots of sailboats on Massachusetts Bay and the impersonal structure of the new John Hancock building towering above the other skyscrapers. Its reflective windows drew the sky and clouds down to itself, giving the building its heightened sense of unreality.

I took a cab from the airport to North Station. Because of the heat, I decided to take the train to my parents' house instead of returning to my apartment. I'd surprise them with a call from the Beverly Farms station. The cabbie was full of enthusiastic questions about my trip, and we talked. We arrived in time for me to catch the six o'clock commuter train. He helped me carry the wannigan, pack, and box of thawing salmon up to the train where I stowed them in the back of a car. I was early. I stood in the shade, leaning against a steel girder, waiting to tell the conductor about my gear.

I could look toward the station and see commuters walking from the sunlight into the shade. With the sun behind them, they appeared to be silhouettes. They looked like the silent shadows reflected on the walls of Plato's cave more than they resembled people. Then one became real. It was my father. He must have been working late. When he came abreast of me, I reached out and touched his shoulder. His look of surprise, and something else, was complete. He spoke first. "You look like a bum," he said, and then he smiled.

In the crowded train we sat across the aisle from each other. We didn't speak, but sat in a comfortable silence. As hot as it was, I knew he wouldn't take off his suit coat, and he didn't. He offered me half his evening paper, but I couldn't concentrate on the news. I was caught up in the ride, one as familiar to me as my name. Even before the conductor called out the stations, I could hear them: Lynn, Salem, Beverly, Monserrat, Prides, Beverly Farms. I watched out the window as we passed the back lots and slag heaps and entered the greener world of the suburbs. The engine's speed sucked the grasses and leafy branches by the tracks in toward the train. I felt I was eavesdropping on my younger self. I thought of the waterfalls.

The papers say there could be as many as 700,000 people in the march today. I've brought my small piece of the tundra, and my hope, with me. Finding the rock this morning, I realized again what I had felt in the cabin with Richard and on the train with my father that evening three years ago. What I'd done hadn't set me apart; it had brought me up against myself, gently, and that remains a constant invitation to put "in order what matters most."

UNGAVA BAY

65°45' 65°30' 65°15' 65°

Rapids
Rapids
Innit
Cabin

58°45'

Korok River

Rapids

Rapi

58°30'

75° 70° 65° 60° 55° 50°

Ungava
Bay
The Palmer-Korok Rivers

60°

LABRADOR
SEA

55°

QUEBEC   LABRADOR

CANADA

50°

NEWFOUNDLAND

Gulf of
St. Lawrence

58°15'

P.E.I.

Montreal

NEW
BRUNSWICK

NOVA SCOTIA

45°

ATLANTIC   OCEAN

Boston

New
York

MILES
0   100   200   300   400   500

0 100 200 300 400 500
KILOMETERS

G.W.WARD

65°45' 65°30' 65°15' 65°